What is IGI?

INVITING G⊕D IN   EDGING G⊕D OUT

IGI

(Pronounced "Iggy")

Refers to:

Inviting God/Good In

Rather than:

EGO

Edging God/Good Out

Read on to learn how to apply The IGI Principles *in your life and business.*

Book Testimonials

"With *The IGI Principles*, my good friend Steve Rodgers has created a powerful book and multimedia experience that distills timeless truths into practical steps and actions that a business owner or leader can apply in their lives. Through his direct and grounded explanations of what to many are nebulous and impractical concepts, Steve is uniquely suited to contribute to the merging of the worlds of business and spirituality."
—John Assaraf, serial entrepreneur, author of two *New York Times* bestselling books, founder and CEO of NeuroGym

"Success is a journey, not a destination. The IGI Principles that Steve Rodgers shares in this book equip and empower readers to be enlightened leaders who put purpose before profit, impact before income. Those who embrace these principles create inspiring corporate cultures that unite teams to deliver massive value in the market, thereby unlocking new levels of profitability and personal fulfillment."
—Brandon Barnum, HOA.com chairman, builder of tech companies for over twenty-three years, and co-founder and former president of Refer.com (now Pod.io)

"Having known Steve personally for several years now, I've long awaited this book. It's the book he was destined to write so that he could share his greatest gift with the world. Steve's gift is showing high-performing business leaders how to apply universal principles of spirituality to great effect in their companies (and personal lives). IGI is a brilliant concept and a best practice business strategy."
—Patrick Combs, international keynote and inspirational speaker, author of *Major in Success* and *Man 1 Bank 0,* which he performed as a one-man show for sold-out audiences around the world

"I have known Steve Rodgers for over a decade—our relationship started around business and through common associations. The more I came in contact with him, the more I realized he was one of those rare people who is as strong in business as he is personally. I've known global leaders of industry and government, and it is a rare person that can blend achievement with a great caring nature and a drive to make business and the world better each day.
—James Conlin, CEO of IAmLife, and CEO/Chairman of Ally Global Services

"Practical and powerful—this is a book that needed to be written! Steve provides a unique guide to operating your business with a spiritual presence. Learn how to invite goodness into your organization, team, and relationships with The IGI Principles!"

—Marshall Goldsmith, New York Times #1 bestselling author of *Triggers, Mojo,* and *What Got You Here Won't Get You There*; Thinkers 50 #1 Executive Coach; and only two-time #1 Leadership Thinker in the world

"*The IGI Principles* could not be released at a better time. Steve shares the importance of the 4 B's, Body, Bonds, Being and *Business, as* a way to live a healthy and abundant life creating a legacy of the highest good."

—Sharon Lechter, CEO of Pay Your Family First, author of *Think and Grow Rich for Women,* and co-author of *Rich Dad Poor Dad, Outwitting the Devil*, and *Three Feet From Gold.*

"A new and far better world is emerging, and Steve Rodgers is right on top of it, leading the way! Finally, in *The IGI Principles*, we have the road map to a happier life in business, as well as personally. Steve's ideas are classic, proven, feel-good principles that lead to success, as well as personal happiness. IGI is a trumpet call to our Higher Selves to come forward and influence our higher, far better lives. Steve Rodgers is an authentic leader in business, as well as in living what he pronounces as the better way. Reading his book, you'll no doubt think, 'I want what he's having!'"

—Shannon Peck, spiritual healer, past life regression counselor, author of *Past Life & Spirit World Regressions: Healing Through Revealing*, and co-founder, with Scott Peck, of *The Love Center*

"If you are looking for how to invite goodness into your life and business, then look no further. *The IGI Principles* by Steve Rodgers will walk you through the whys and hows of his method that will ultimately lead you to opening yourself up for personal and professional success, abundance, and fulfillment."

—Jessica Rhodes, Founder of Interview Connections, the first and top podcast booking service

"One of those books that leaves you better off for reading it. LOVE this message. Perfect for today's society."

—Greg S. Reid, serial entrepreneur, speaker, and author of the Think and Grow Rich series and the Secret Knock Workshops

"The concept of the IGI Principles has been coming to the world and forming for many years and we are blessed to have this amazing book making its debut now. I absolutely love the entire concept of the IGI Principles, and knowing Steve Rodgers, there is no one better to bring this concept to us. He not only put these life-changing principles in a format for the world to embrace and easily enjoy, he also lives his life as an example of the principles he teaches.
—Eileen Schwartz, founder and owner of The Impact Principle and certified trainer, speaker and coach

"Steve Rodgers shares his wisdom, courage, and golden nuggets of how to live a generous, grateful, and forgiving life. In this most challenging time, this book is very much needed in the world. Going within is the only way to access the clarity and brighter side of life. Thank you, Steve, for this gift!"
—Nancy Spears, CEO at GenConnect and author of *Buddha: 9 to 5: The Eightfold Path to Enlightening Your Workplace and Improving Your Bottom Line*

"Steve Rodgers Invites GOodness in. In doing so, he reverses the ego from Edging Out to Inviting In. Steve has revealed the powerful secret of the recognition of ego and the transmutation of ego energy into gold in creating relationships that take the reader into a complete paradigm shift that takes the infinite energy of goodness, creates a new partner relationship, and takes trust to unbelievable new heights. Well worth the investment of time to learn Steve's remarkable secret of manifesting goodness. Congratulations and thank you for sharing your goodness and GODNESS."
—Brian Sidorsky, founder and CEO of Lansdowne Equity Ventures Ltd

"*The IGI Principles* is a humbling deep dive and inner journey into your self that helps you better understand how to attract and retain all the goodness that's coming to you without pushing it away. Your ego is a huge blockage, and Steve's masterful work walks you down the path to better align your mission and mindset. The Power of Gratitude, among other chapters, can't be overstated. Steve's authentic and highly genuine wisdom comes from his own experiences. This is a book I will be sure to read every few years to remind myself of the IGI Principles and to live and lead a better life filled with purpose, love, and fulfillment."
—David Tal, former real estate executive, marketing pro, and co-founder of Verse

"This is a warm, wonderful book, full of ideas and insights that will open your mind and heart to the true potential that lies within you. Not only is it a joy to read, but you will never be the same afterward."
—Brian Tracy, author of over seventy bestselling books, consultant to over 1,000 companies, and international speaker

"Very few human beings that I have met in this life are able to articulate "the art of the heart" of how to live a God centered life in the maelstrom of human existence than my friend Steve Rogers. In his book "The IGI Principles" he presents a step by step process of how to integrate the eternal life giving principles of Truth into all our earth affairs -- business, social, and family.
What divine timing! "The IGI Principles" are here just in the nick of time for every being seeking a deeper relationship with their Creator and the awakening of the GOOD within themselves and our global family."
—Reverend Tom Kelly, yoga teacher, prior monk, coach, teacher, love master and prior Co-Owner of Soul of Yoga.

Sign up for my email list to receive more IGI content to transform your personal and professional life: http://aha.pub/WheelsOfLife

By signing up now, you will receive a downloadable and printable Wheel of Life diagram to self-assess your health and success in all aspects of your life, including your Body, Bonds, Business, and Being.

You will also have access to even more of my future valuable IGI items that can help you on your journey.

Scan the QR code or use this link to watch the call to action video: https://steverodgers.net/call-to-action

The IGI Principles

The Power of Inviting Good In vs Edging Good Out

Steve Rodgers

THiNKaha®

An Actionable Success Journal

E-mail: info@thinkaha.com
20660 Stevens Creek Blvd., Suite 210
Cupertino, CA 95014

Please go to
https://aha.pub/IGIPrinciples
to read this AHAbook and to share the
individual AHAmessages that resonate with you.

Published by THiNKaha®
20660 Stevens Creek Blvd., Suite 210,
Cupertino, CA 95014
https://thinkaha.com
E-mail: info@thinkaha.com

First Printing: September 2020
Hardcover ISBN: 978-1-61699-369-6   1-61699-369-3
Paperback ISBN: 978-1-61699-368-9   1-61699-368-5
eBook ISBN: 978-1-61699-367-2   1-61699-367-7
Place of Publication: Silicon Valley, California, USA
Paperback Library of Congress Number: 2020909429

Dedication

To God, the source and the energy of everything.

Acknowledgements

"If the only prayer you ever say in your entire life is thank you, it will be enough."
—Meister Eckhart

I have many people to thank for their influence in my life and their support of this book. As gratitude is one of the most essential elements of the IGI formula and to keeping the flow of goodness circulating in our lives, I try my best to share my praise as much as I can but recognize that I can always do more.

There are many more people to express my gratitude than I have the time or space to include in this book. Even if I don't mention you here, know that if we have come into contact, then I have learned from you and benefitted from your kindness, wisdom, and generosity or been inspired by you in some way. I have also added an "Ambassadors" section at the end of the book for those individuals who have supported and spread the message of this book and who I would highly recommend the reader research to see how they can be of help to you.

First, I wish to recognize my wife, Mary Lou, who for over thirty years, has always been beside me with total love and support. She is living her own unique version of IGI by helping women with addiction in the sober living space, while sharing any free moments with our grandkids, who light up her face and fill her heart.

My parents, Al and Jackie Rodgers, who were my first teachers of IGI, not so much in their words but by their actions and the way they lived their life as an example of individuals who do the right thing.

My children, Nicole and PJ, and my grandkids, Ema, Sarah, Cove, and Dezi, who have helped brighten my life and bring me much more joy than I could have expected on this journey.

Also, my brothers, Jay, Barry, Mike, and Kenny, the guys who always poked and prodded me with that unique brotherly love that caused me to find even more inner strength and acceptance.

A special shoutout to my sister-in-law, Eileen Schwartz, who has been a great advocate and cheerleader for me. She even named her dog IGI ten years ago, and he has been the unofficial mascot of the movement but is soon to be official. And speaking of cheerleaders, there are few cheering louder for me than my mother-in-law, Dolores Schreiber-Pugh, who is one of my biggest fans. I love her for her belief in me and for the many gifts she brings to others.

I want to acknowledge, as always, my friends and mentors in my professional work who have helped shape more of who I am today as a man and as a leader. Foremost among these is Mark Thompson, who generously wrote the foreword of this book. Mark is not only an inspiration and role model for many in the business world, but he is also one to me personally. He is an example of a servant leader with a big heart in all that he does in the world. Others who support and inspire me are Brian Tracy, Marshall Goldsmith, Dr. Bernard Meltzer, John Assaraf, and Jim Bunch, among others too many to name.

I also want to give a special mention of Gary Ranker, who passed away last year. Just as I work and help others around the themes of transformation, evolution, and transition, he transitioned last year into a totally new experience. May his soul soar high and wide.

I'm grateful to Seth Balthazar for joining my team recently in helping to bring my words to life and fill in the gaps of my ideas and writing, as well as to Mitchell Levy and his team at AHAthat, who have published this book and done so much to make it as effective and helpful as possible for the reader. Additionally, I'd like to honor a full-circle moment in life and thank Jill Menius Cameron for her help with proofreading and edits. This time it was much more appreciated than 20 years ago when she did a surprise edit of one of my emails. I was not near as grateful then as I am now!

Brian Sidorsky, whom I met a few years ago and was instrumental in my involvement with the Global Junior Achievement organization. Brian has been a model of the power of doing good work and Inviting Good Into the world.

I want to give a shout-out to two childhood friends I've known since I was a teenager and continue to be great friends with, along with their families: Tracy Jefferson and her husband, Rob, and Heather Waites and her husband, Kevin. Both continue to inspire me with friendship, fun, and remembering the importance of what life is all about.

Also, gratitude to Tom Kelly, a personal spiritual advisor, who along with his wife, founded Soul of Yoga, my yoga studio now for many years. From Tom, I have received much guidance and teaching in the deep practice of living in IGI.

Thanks to Dimitri Kozlov, who owns Influex, the company that built my new website, and his team of David Munter and Kenney Knipes, who did such a great job on it.

I wish to recognize Patrick Combs, a friend, an associate, my origin story writer, and my speaking coach, who along with Eric Lochtefeld, leads the Bliss Mastermind course that I did for a year, which has been instrumental in my own personal growth and evolution.

Eric Magna, for his stellar video work, and Monique Feil, for expertly capturing me with her photography skills.

Thanks to Asheesh Advani, CEO of Junior Achievement Global, whom I met early on when I got involved with JA. Also, Margie Wang, who was the CFO of JA Global and has been especially instrumental in my life in the last couple of years.

Andrew Hewitt of Gamechangers 500 is someone I highly respect and from whom I have modeled some of my IGI ideas for a future integrated business platform that can work to serve businesses at a higher level.

I wish to express my gratitude to the array of clients whom I've been working with both in the past and present and exploring business strategies and the IGI principles with for years in our private conversations together. A few among these are Paul Morris, Eddy Krifcher and the leadership team of Keller Williams, Eric Spitz of MyNHD, James Conlin from IAM LIFE, Mo Ranji of Roya, and David and Avi Tal of Verse, formerly Agentology.

I often reflect on the quote from my first book, *Lead to Gold*, which says, "Breaking through resistance is the price you pay for the dream you say you want." In my life, I have been on an inner quest to seek, explore, learn, read, experience, travel, question, meditate, and pray for ways to find my own path and create my own personal legend. On that journey, I have broken through much fear and resistance to find the great power that lies on the other side of fear. This book has only come about through the breaking down of the walls and barriers in my own mind and ego so I can express my own IGI and share it with others.

For that inspiration and guidance for my ongoing lifelong journey, I feel immense gratitude to God, the Divine Source, and all the master teachers who are extensions of God, such as Jesus Christ, Buddha, Mohammed, Krishna, and Paramahansa Yogananda, along with all the other messengers and teachers of God in my life, in whatever form they have appeared.

Testimonial

This type of shout-out is not something you typically see in a book. It's here because I want to highlight an example of IGI that truly stands out.

Encounters with individuals like Mitchell Levy don't happen as often as they should. This book is here because Mitchell and his team helped me give birth to my life's work.

This is no small feat. My brain, my thoughts, my plans for what I want to accomplish with this book, and my efforts are huge, which makes it hard for me to simplify and focus on what should go into this volume and what might go into the next one.

The service, support, and friendship I received from Mitchell went well beyond what I expected. He saw my struggle with using the concept of God vs. spirit, as well the focus on corporate vs. personal, and provided opportunities for me to think about, react to, and focus my energies for this book. For that, I am so grateful and wanted to express my appreciation beyond just saying, "Thank you!"

If you need help pulling out your genius and turning it into a book that will help you increase your credibility, reach out to Mitchell and his team.

Scan the bar code or click on the link below to watch a video shout-out to Mitchell as well.

http://aha.pub/SteveRodgers-Testimonial

A THiNKaha book is not your typical book. It's a whole lot more while being a whole lot less. Scan the QR code or use this link to watch Mitchell Levy talk about this new evolutionary style of book: https://aha.pub/THiNKahaSeries

How to Read a THiNKaha® Book
A Note from the Publisher

The AHAthat/THiNKaha series was crafted to deliver content the way humans process information in today's world. Short, sweet, and to the point while delivering powerful, lasting impact.

The content is designed and presented in ways to appeal to visual, auditory, and kinesthetic personality types. Each section contains AHAmessages, lines for notes, and a meme that summarizes that section. You should also scan the QR code, or click on the link, to watch a video of the author talking about that section.

This book is contextual in nature. Although the words won't change, their meaning will every time you read it as your context will. Be ready, you will experience your own AHA moments as you read. The AHA messages are designed to be stand-alone actionable messages that will help you think differently. Items to consider as you're reading include:

1. When you're reading, write one to three action items that resonate with you in the underlined areas.
2. Mark your calendar to re-read it again.
3. Repeat step #1 and mark one to three additional AHA messages that resonate. As they will most likely be different, this is a great time to reflect on the messages that resonated with you during your last reading.
4. Sprinkle credust on the author and yourself by sharing the AHA messages from this book socially from the AHAthat platform https://aha.pub/IGIPrinciples.

After reading this THiNKaha book, marking your AHA messages, rereading it, and marking more AHA messages, you'll begin to see how this book contextually applies to you. We advocate for continuous, lifelong learning and this book will help you transform your AHAs into action items with tangible results.

Mitchell Levy, Global Credibility Expert
publisher@thinkaha.com

THiNKaha®

Contents

Foreword by Mark C. Thompson

I'm so excited to have the opportunity to support Steve in this journey that he's taking people on to find their higher self in the work that they do and to manifest the dreams that they have wanted all their lives. They can do this because they've learned something fresh along the way that's allowed them to become more than they ever imagined possible.

Steve has a remarkable method presented in this book that he has shared with me and all the people who have been touched throughout the world by his message, both in his keynote presentations and in his administration, management, and entrepreneurship of some of the greatest brands in the world.

I remember when he was helping support one of Warren Buffet's noteworthy companies. Steve has always been a man who loves people more than he loves profit, a man who believes that the only path to profit is through allowing an individual, an organization, and a team to rally around that common spirit they can only form when they believe that they are loved, supported, valued, admired, and respected. That's something that he has done under the greatest stress, under the greatest challenges, and in circumstances that have been less ideal than you might imagine.

When we see the work being done by great thought leaders, authors, and executives like Steve, we think that they come from privilege, that they have somehow had special access, a platform, the wind at their back, or the capacity to somehow harness other people's money so they wouldn't have to be at risk. Certainly, Steve, like so many of us, has been able to be successful not through having any special privilege but by helping others create a life that matters, by helping them find that higher mojo, that sense of purpose, and that passion that turns into performance.

The thing that drives Steve and the work that he's going to share with you in this book is the sensibility of bringing the entire human experience into the impact that you can deliver for a company. Imagine if you could bring everything that you've known and done into focus so you can create a structure to manifest that next chapter in your life, in your work, in your relationships, and in the long-term legacy that you want to build.

I get a sense of pride in having the opportunity to meet with so many profoundly gifted entrepreneurs around the world. I've worked with the Virgin Group and Richard Branson as he has reinvented company after company with both technology and a kind of sexy, fresh, youthful vibe. I've had the opportunity to work with unicorns, Lyft and Pinterest, who created a whole business model around finding your passion, diving deep into it, and commercializing that. What we're seeing here is person after person who's been touched by the methods that you'll see in this book and who has been able to transform, in the true sense of the word, and find a way forward that allows them to bring their whole self to that process.

I can't wait for you to dive into each page or even jump back and forth when you need to be inspired in a specific capacity. The way this book is organized makes that more eminently possible by using technology that allows you to jump in and see videos, feel connected with the concept, and revisit that over and over again. You don't have to worry about getting this in sequence. It's all about you finding the value. That's why the book has been organized in this way. This element truly makes it an interactive experience where you feel as though you are sitting down and talking with one of the great leaders in the business world today.

Steve and his team have come together to bring about what I think will be one of the most meaningful adventures you'll ever take in your career. I look forward to hearing about how that journey has gone for all of you.

—Mark C. Thompson

World's #1 CEO coach, serial Midas Touch investor, former chief of staff of Charles Schwab, *New York Times* bestselling author, serial Broadway show producer, and international keynote speaker

Scan the QR code or use this link to watch the foreword video:
https://steverodgers.net/foreword-by-mark-thompson

Introduction

EGO is Edging GOod Out
IGI is Inviting GOod In

This simple truth is the fundamental message of this book: by inviting goodness into our life, and living as an open-hearted offering of service, we open ourselves to unimagined personal and professional success, abundance, and fulfillment.

The genesis of this book has been many years in the making. Having spent decades in the corporate and business world, I have seen first-hand how all too many entrepreneurs and leaders become obsessed with the bottom line of profit at all costs. In the process, these individuals may harm their relationships with others, fail to serve the greater good of humanity, and ultimately leaves them unfulfilled. This disconnect is because their work in the world is not informed by their soul's true purpose. Luckily, others are aiding their community while seeing some measure of business success. However, these leaders also know there are always ways to improve, expand their knowledge, and create more gifts through which others can benefit.

For a long time, ideas have been forming in my mind as to how to bring a spiritual consciousness into the business sphere. Years ago, when the flash of inspiration about IGI (pronounced "iggy") hit me, I bought web domains and even registered the book title as I knew that someday I would write a book with that title and on that subject. Now, many years later, this is that book!

In my late 30s, I was experiencing career success as the president of a large, nationally known, real estate company. I was appointed to lead the multi-billion dollar company owned by Berkshire Hathaway, by a close appointed executive of Warren Buffett. Simultaneously, my health and relationships were deteriorating due to my lifelong addiction to alcohol. An addiction that I succumbed to because of my ravenous desire for more. An addiction I chased to fill the "hole in my soul". I then realized I was seeking a sense of purpose, a "deeper meaning" in my life but could not yet find a way to fulfill it with what the world could offer.

Alcohol was one of many earthly, human and material indulgences I pursued that provided a temporary thrill, but after the glitter wore off, it left me unfulfilled. I was seeking a profound feeling of peace, of home, of love, and of deep fulfilment, that comes with living a life guided by one's soul purpose. Eventually the effect my drinking was having on my relationships and health, caused me to make a radical change of consciousness. I dedicated myself to living in a totally different way.

Over time, the challenges in my life cracked the shell of my ego and I was left with no choice but to surrender. I had to allow a deeper intelligence to guide my life. I always believed in the influence of a higher power and had been on a spiritual quest since my late teens, but this was now pushed into a whole new level. The change I underwent was to stop attempting to selfishly fill the hole in my soul, through harmful self-pleasures, possessions, experiences, and material success. Now I would live my life as an act of service for all.

I have successfully run multi-billion dollar businesses, sat at high-profile corporate tables in executive roles, spoken to the needs of shareholders of some of the world's largest corporations, and owned and operated my own companies. In short, I have walked the walk in the highly-competitive world of business. As a result, the ideas I share here are not airy-fairy, feel-good spiritual platitudes – they are essential practices that are a valuable guidance for anyone seeking to evolve to their highest good in both business and life.

I don't consider myself a guru or to have any spiritual authority. However, I am a man who has extensive experience, and success, in diverse businesses. I have discovered my purpose and unique gift, to bring a greater consciousness and Spiritual Intelligence into the business world. I do this all while understanding the competitive environment of the business sphere, and the high demand for profits that those within it must manage.

My journey has taken me to this place today, and I realize I can no longer hold the principles in this book back. From my extensive years of business experience, I came to realize I yearned to give birth to IGI and share it with others. These ideas have been calling to me, and I am thankful to be the person who is merely a vehicle for their message. I now fondly refer to myself as a "Spiritual Business Activist" and my style as "Excutive Zen".

This is my calling and I believe that this is a message that the world needs at this time. The Earth needs businesses that are sustainable, respectful of humanity, and purpose-driven, to serve the greater good. We require businesses that, at their core, are for benefit, rather than just for profit. And the great news is that by serving the greater good of all, you are rewarded with all the abundance you and your businesses desire.

It is my intention to help lead an IGI movement in the world where more and more people are empowered to invite in a deeper Spiritual Intelligence in every aspect of their lives. However, before a movement can start, we first need to know how to say the key word! Many people are unfamiliar with IGI the first time they read it. IGI is pronounced "iggy", similar to "jiggy" as coined in the late 90's Will Smith song "Gettin' Jiggy Wit It." So now, in addition to "getting jiggy with it", we can also "get IGI with it!"

I hope that you find the things I will share with you in this book helpful, and you apply them in your life and business to reap great rewards. The results you will discover are not just in profits, but in relationships; not just in dollars, but also in that which is priceless - living each day in the deep joy of fulfilling your sacred purpose in your life.

In our world, the word "profit" will soon come to have a much deeper meaning. Just as the word "abundance" can refer to being rich and sufficient in all areas of one's life. Our definition of "profit" can likewise expand beyond financial profits to all things that benefit the whole.

Let's begin our journey together of Inviting GOodness Into every area of your business and life.

Scan the QR code or use this link to watch the introduction
video: https://steverodgers.net/introduction

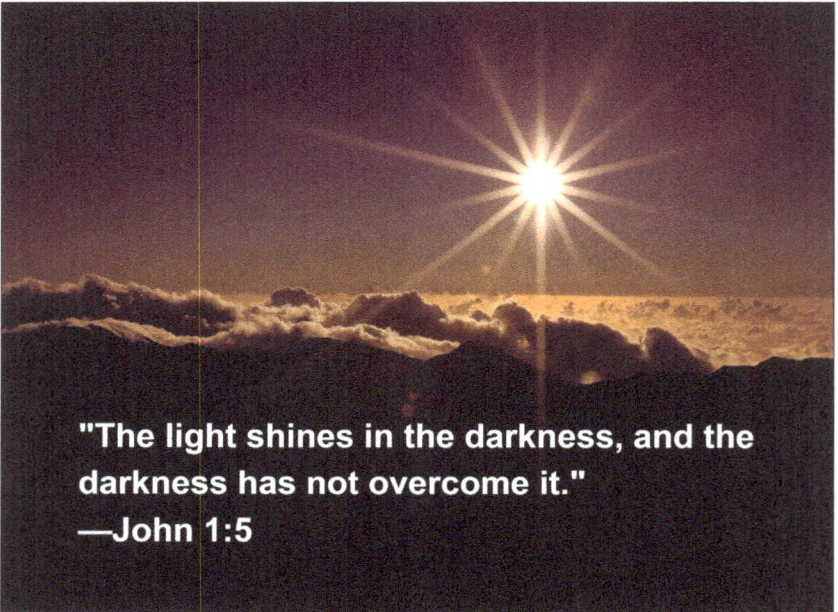

"The light shines in the darkness, and the darkness has not overcome it."
—John 1:5

Steve Rodgers
https://aha.pub/IGIPrinciples

A Tale of Two Viruses

As this book is going to print in the summer of 2020, recent events have inspired me to add this section. I am compelled to address the two challenging events that are deeply affecting every individual, and shaking our society to the core.

The coronavirus worldwide pandemic and the George Floyd murder, have ignited America and many other countries, into mass protests against injustice in all forms. As I see it, we are simultaneously battling two viruses: the physical virus of COVID-19 and the far more dangerous virus of inequality.

While the advocacy for freedom and dignity of Black Americans is at the forefront of Black Lives Matter, these protests go much deeper. George Floyd is only one of far too many individuals, known and unknown, who have been victimized by the systemic racism in our society.

The Black Lives Matter protests are the expression of the anger, the pain, and the frustration of millions of people. These people represent all different races, ideologies, and life experiences, collectively taking action to *demand* change.

For millennia, there has been vast inequality and oppression of those at the bottom rung of the ladder in society. Those with wealth and power have exploited those of lesser means, to achieve their own ends; often not even recognizing the innate divinity or common humanity of those they oppress. While the United States, and the world as a whole, have taken significant steps to provide equality for all, the truth is that we still have a significant way to go to live in a world where everyone is free to live equally.

Just like the coronavirus, the discriminatory virus is highly contagious. It spreads when we identify only with our ego, and so, are blinded from our greater spiritual reality and unity with all other beings. We think we are only our physical form, that we are our name, and our history. We then identify as separate from others, and must be violent toward them in order to protect ourselves. In extreme cases, we see others only as a means to an end, a resource to exploit.

This highly separative consciousness is what has created our current world of such oppression, suppression, and conflict. If believing in separation and living in ego consciousness (*Edging God Out*) is the problem, then naturally understanding our true nature as ultimately as one and living in IGI (*Inviting God In*) is the solution.

I am a firm believer in the power of positivity, and that all things can be transformed into a benefit, no matter how grim they may seem. With both the coronavirus and Black Lives Matter movement, there is the opportunity to descend into despair and bitterness. However, there are signs and examples of positivity and hope everywhere you look. Individuals all over the world affirm humanity's fundamental goodness, in their actions that spring from love and integrity.

What we are collectively fighting for is to affirm the value of all life and all beings. As we express our freedoms, we create ripple effects for others, both expectedly and unexpectedly. Some of these ripples will have negative consequences. Perhaps this is a lesson of the universe: every action has an equal and opposite reaction.

We have the right to speak and march to take action against inequality, discrimination and systemic racism. However, while protesting is our right, we have a responsibility to keep our society healthy and safe. The risk of passing the coronavirus in large crowds is a serious concern.

Above all, we must remember that when you fight fire with fire, you only get more fire. When you fight hate with hate, it only inflames the fire of hate. Therefore, we must find ways to stay in IGI and not to succumb to anger and outrage.

It may seem as if there is so much injustice in our world, and there is! However, this has been present for thousands of years of human history. Presently, people are finally seeing the darkness that has been buried in our societal structures and institutions, as well as in each one of us. By bringing the injustices in our world out from under the rug and onto the table, we can collectively decide what we want to keep, and what can be thrown away as the product of old beliefs. By bringing this unconscious darkness and shadow into clear awareness, we are able to transform it into light.

We exist in a transformational age on planet Earth. This process of looking within to see what has been denied, suppressed, and neglected is happening on the collective level, and on the individual level simultaneously. We are seeing worldwide movements, like #MeToo and Black Lives Matter, that voice the cries of many. Individuals are experiencing their own personal confrontation with their shadows, as they are being offered the opportunity to transform and transcend their limited consciousness. Only then, are they able to evolve along with the evolution of humanity as a whole.

It is fundamental to march in the streets, taking action in your daily life to advocate for the values you believe in and the world you know is possible. It is equally important to examine your thoughts and beliefs, to honestly look within and see where in your mind may reside unconscious judgments, hidden fears, and suppressed traumas. As you heal yourself and bring more light to the darkness, you share your energy and your inner harmony with the world. This is what the world needs more than anything: individuals who are inwardly whole and who are creating a new Earth out of positivity, joy, and love, rather than merely fighting against the old world out of pain and anger.

There are no coincidences, and I am amazed at the grand plan and synchronicity that has led to this book being published in the midst of these highly chaotic times. The IGI principles in this book can aid you in living an integrated and harmonious life in all aspects. They will assist you in living from the deepest part of your being, so you can express your most compassionate and wise version of yourself.

This is applied in all aspects of your life, for that is the point of IGI. You live and express yourself as one whole being in your personal and professional lives, and you fulfill your piece of the puzzle that contributes to building a new world for all.

So, these two events, along with what will surely be more challenging and highly charged worldwide events in our future, are experiences where we are offered the great opportunity to practice *Inviting God and Goodness In*. We are not to be drawn into the drama of the ego, which seeks to fight, create polarization, and inflame the fires of hate.

What is the answer to the challenges in our world today? I have offered a few thoughts, but the answer is still to be decided by us all. However, individuals such as Gandhi and Martin Luther King Jr. provided examples of the power of loving, non-violent resistance to oppression, while creating new systems to replace the old.

As Dr. King said: "Darkness cannot drive out darkness; only light can do that. Hate cannot drive out hate; only love can do that."

By being positive and peaceful in your state of IGI, you keep yourself always in the eye of the storm, where all is calm even though chaos may be swirling all around you. You will be a beacon of clarity in the foggy night and tumultuous waves for everyone around you, showing them that they, too, can simply *Invite God In* and find that inner peace and guidance.

"The main problem with listening to EGO is that you're always caught in the trap of striving and never arriving. Thus, you can never feel whole and complete." —Wayne Dyer

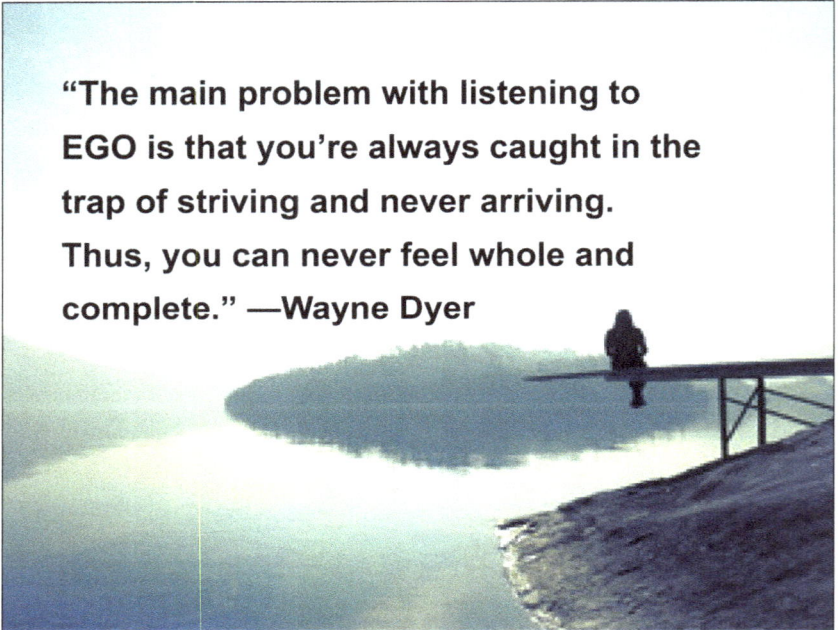

Steve Rodgers
https://aha.pub/IGIPrinciples

At the very end of this section, share the AHA messages from this book socially by going to **https://aha.pub/IGIPrinciples**.

Section I

Inviting Good In VS Edging Good Out

In the past, success in life and in business was all about making money. Times have changed. In today's world, success is also about creating, sharing, and inspiring goodness internally and externally.

Business owners and leaders would greatly benefit by seeking more understanding that all stakeholders in their businesses are key contributors to achieving success. *Inviting GOodness In* can help create a culture of happiness and success. This radiates out into immediate communities and the world. The concept of viral didn't start with social media or a digital media post, its original source was the heart and spirit.

Nowadays, people look for socially-conscious leaders, who are not raiding the planet and squeezing every nickel from their customers. People don't want to do business with someone who only wants to make money. Entrepreneurs and bosses who focus primarily on making money won't keep their customers—even with the best products or services.

Many business leaders may have originally started out thinking of doing good, but somewhere along the way profit rolled in and had to be achieved at all cost. The idea of serving others to make this world a better place was, at times, pushed away.

The future of the business world is clear: companies must be acting in integrity and serve the best interests of their employees, their customers, their stakeholders, and the Earth as a whole. No longer, can a company make massive profits while destroying the environment and exploiting people. The successful entrepreneurs of today, and the future, are those who create and lead companies that are financially successful and conscious in all aspects of their operation. Consciousness must be present financially, socially, environmentally, and spiritually. The great news is that the more goodness is invited into business, the more success is allowed in as well.

In this section, readers can find out the value of doing good for others instead of just selfishly fulfilling their own needs and desires. The discussion focuses on the difference between IGI (*Inviting GOod In*) and EGO (*Edging GOod Out*). IGI-oriented leaders need to identify where their focus is. How does *Edging Good Out* affect their lives and businesses? Is there a way to create a balance between the two? Is there a way to implant the IGI Principles in one's business, not just your personal life? Can business owners use the IGI Principles to attract customers and retain employees, and make even more profits? How?

There are many definitions of what defines the ego, but one of the most succinct is from Wayne Dyer, in which he referred to ego as E.G.O, or "Edging God Out." This definition directly reveals how our self-obsession closes us off from the higher power and intelligence that is all around us, and is the very source of our existence. We become like a tree without roots, disconnected from the source of our own life.

I think his explanation of the six components of the ego is worth looking at in light of that definition.

According to Dyer, this is what ego says:

1. I am what I have.
2. I am what I do.
3. I am what other people think of me.
4. I am separate from everybody else.
5. I am separate from what is missing in my life.
6. I am separate from God or Source.

If we reverse these statements and reflect on what IGI, *Inviting Good In*, could be as a mirror image of these six beliefs, we can start to think of it like this:

1. I am not what I have.
2. I am not what I do.
3. I am not what other people think of me.
4. I am not separate from everyone else.
5. I am not separate from what is missing in my life.
6. I am not separate from God or Source.

In considering a definition of God as "the Sum of All That Is," we can consider and possibly accept that we are part of Source as a smaller piece of God. Just as if you were to take a clear large glass, stand in the waves of the ocean and bend down, scooping out a full glass of ocean water, is that water still not part of the ocean source from which it came? And as you empty out your glass of ocean water, back to the source from which it came, it then flows fully back into the whole of the ocean, leaving behind the smaller space that it took for but a few moments.

This, in the most simplistic way, is how I view life, the source of life, and how all flows from that source, is the sum of All That Is. We are all nothing more than energy in various levels of vibration, that takes the form of matter, mind, intelligence, and higher evolved states.

This energy and life force ebbs and flows as the world, and our lives, play out daily in all of our interactions and experiences. The question is: how will you manifest your own energy in each and every hour of the day? Do you choose to live in ego, or perhaps now, in even more IGI?

Where ego isolates a person from existence by the false belief that they are separate from everyone and everything else, IGI is a reminder that each individual is intimately connected with all of creation. Where we once pushed goodness out in our ignorance, we now *Invite GOodness In* because we understand the power of surrender, and allowing our life to be informed by a deeper purpose.

A ship without a course is one that wanders around and gets lost upon the ocean. A business owner must know the deeper purpose of their life. Being aligned with the soul's purpose is like having a strong wind blowing in one's sails, that always provides the energy and inspiration needed to move forward successfully.

This section challenges business owners and leaders to not be afraid to ask questions such as:

- Who am I?
- Why am I here?
- How can I live my Highest Good?
- How can I make an even bigger positive impact?

When they understand how to better themselves by beginning to ask these questions, it opens the door for endless possibilities to *Invite Good In*. Their understanding of who they are and their purpose in this life becomes bigger than themselves. That knowledge and realization can impact their business and can trickle down to everything they do, and the people around them. This impact extends not only to their business, but also to their personal lives, their families, their community, and therefore, the world they live in.

Inviting GOoD In helps carry the message of how important it is that IGI-oriented leaders are human beings first, and a business person second. IGI expands someone's purpose so they can begin to assess themselves and ask, "Whom can I help make a difference for?" IGI-driven owners are not afraid to stay on track and maximize what they are doing, consistently evaluating where they are at, where they are going, and what they can do to accelerate growth, not only for business's sake but also to consider adding value to their personnel.

IGI helps entrepreneurs have better connections with employees, their customers, and potentially, their products and services. The ripple effect produces good and harmonious relationships in the workplace, in the community, and in the world. The IGI principles aids in bettering organizations and increasing their scalability.

As such, owners and executives can maximize their ecosystems, processes, and structures that work even better, and with more sustainability. When companies are set up to *Invite Good In*, there's no better environment conducive for creativity, productivity, and collaboration at work.

Many entrepreneurs were taught to be aggressive, cutthroat, driven, and competitive in order to be successful. They consciously, or unconsciously, make decisions based on how they're going to benefit from a situation, how they're going to get more out of it, and how they can win over a person. That, in a nutshell, is what ego is—something that only serves one's self and undermines the welfare of others. That mindset might get them on top of the food chain, but is it good for their lives and businesses in the long run?

Ego can easily manifest when owners are only serving themselves. Are they making choices that only serve to increase their own power at the expense of others? It's a self-satisfying principle, that focuses on getting and receiving, without giving and aiding others in equal measure. When they are ego-centric, they are essentially *Edging GOodness Out*.

On the other hand, IGI is about servant leadership, which is anchored in one's consciousness and intentionality to serve others. If ego is all about getting and receiving personal satisfaction, IGI is centered on creating for others and serving everyone possible, in each situation, and as a whole.

The greatest leaders are those who lead not for their personal ego gratification but to serve the greater good of all. They are servants who ensure that everyone is supported and empowered to reach their highest potential.

Being a leader means taking charge, evaluating the situation, making decisions, and directing others. It can, therefore, be difficult to balance the instinct to command, the necessity of listening, and the need to have a strong ego that believes in oneself, and one's vision. While also asking for and receiving advice from others.

The true leader asks themselves: "Whom do I serve?" They serve the highest good and invite that guidance into their own life, so they may then guide others. The true leader is a servant; they are put in a place of leadership because they are exceptionally qualified to listen to the needs of everyone and make decisions that are best for the whole group. They view their role with great humility and responsibility.

Truth be told, human beings can actually have a healthy ego—through having the drive for success, a healthy self-esteem, and strong confidence. How can owners and leaders stay out of the negative ego mindset? It is through IGI: *Inviting Good In*. Every breath, every word, every action, every deed ingrained in their being, to *Invite Good In*, will result in good business decisions. Entrepreneurs applying the IGI Principles consciously find ways to incorporate what they believe in. Whether this be in the way they think, the way they talk to colleagues and employees, or the way they respond to challenging situations in the workplace.

IGI is about giving and creating for others, contrary to ego, which is purely doing things for themselves. When business leaders *Invite Good In*, it allows them to entirely be their authentic selves. IGI acknowledges there is a bigger entity, there is a higher purpose and meaning in our lives.

Artificial intelligence is much talked about today, but it is spiritual intelligence that is desperately needed. Spiritual intelligence is far from artificial; it is completely natural and innate. Without spiritual intelligence, a business can only be marginally successful in an external and limited way. Spiritual intelligence is holistic; it sees the whole of life and so understands how everything fits together. It is also infinitely deep, because it exists when individuals and businesses are connected to the higher power that is the source of everything. Finally, spiritual intelligence is loving, in that it supports and values each individual.

When applied to business, implementing spiritual intelligence brings the benefits of depth, integrity, compassion, and holistic action to bear in all that individuals do. Spiritual intelligence knows the wisdom of letting go, surrendering, and trusting in the flow of life. In doing this, businesses and entrepreneurs are able to grow and evolve without the limitations of the fearful, controlling, egoic mind.

Every religion may have its own version of a higher entity (God, Mother Nature, Chi, etc.). Essentially, every owner and leader has their own commitment—their own covenant and personal spirituality—that they don't need to impose on others. However, when asked what drives them, they can say that their energy is doing good and can be seen in making decisions to connect with new clients, take on new projects, etc.

Owners and leaders can incorporate IGI as a personal covenant in their lives by consciously choosing the welfare of others before themselves. Whether it's meeting people, having a conversation with employees or partners, signing a contract, or deciding whether to give into vices, they can consciously make those decisions based on their commitment to *Invite Good In*. IGI may require a strong faith in a power greater than one's self, but that isn't difficult if one acknowledges that the greater power always knows, ultimately, what is best.

The IGI Principles are the truth that *Inviting GOodness In* is the only way to truly live. As human beings, we are, at every moment, being offered the same choice: either to isolate ourselves from existence through living in fear, greed, lack, and judgment— or to open up to our connection with existence through surrender, forgiveness, gratitude, love, and abundance.

Each moment leaders, and all people, are either *Edging Good Out* or *Inviting Good In*. This is their choice, and they are always receiving the fruits of their choices. The IGI Principles are a reminder to take a moment, to listen within, to one's inner orientation, the higher source, and to where one is coming from with each thought and action in our lives.

Scan the QR code or use this link to watch the section videos and more on this section topic:
https://steverodgers.net/inviting-good-in-vs-edging-good-out

1

There is a power greater than ourselves (e.g., God, Mother Nature, the universe, etc.) that wants you to do good things and to be a better person and leader. Are you opening yourself up for this power to help you achieve #BusinessSuccess? #InviteGoodIn

_____

_____

2

When you fill your soul with more goodness and positivity, you can become a better leader and a better person. #InviteGoodIn

_____

_____

_____

3

#Spiritual intelligence is key to achieving a consistently growing, evolving, successful, and vibrant business. Are you creating spiritual intelligence within your business and life? #InviteGoodIn #BusinessSuccess

_____

_____

_____

4

Edging good out is self-serving vs. inviting good in is all about serving people other than yourself. Who are you serving more in your business and communities? #BusinessSuccess

_____

_____

_____

5

Edging good out and being self-serving can sometimes be a necessary component of success, but doing that too often can have negative results for you. Remember to still #InviteGoodIn to maintain balance in your life and business. #BusinessSuccess

_____

_____

_____

6

Businesses that are only focused on making money:
1) won't keep employees for long and 2) won't attract long-
term customers despite having good products/services.
#InviteGoodIn #BusinessSuccess

_____

_____

_____

7

Many successful businesses operate to serve and help
other businesses, other people, and communities
instead of operating only to make money. How does your
business operate? #InviteGoodIn #BusinessSuccess

_____

_____

_____

8

The decisions you make in your businesses should aid everyone in it whenever possible. These decisions often bring greater positive results. #InviteGoodIn #BusinessSuccess

_____

_____

_____

9

Employees and customers want a business that is:
1) socially conscious and 2) true to its good mission
statement. Is your business a place people want to work in
and do business with? #InviteGoodIn #BusinessSuccess

_____

_____

_____

10

Your good core values, vision statements, and
mission statements should not just be plaques on
the walls. Make sure you incorporate these acts in
everything your business is doing at all levels to achieve
#BusinessSuccess. #InviteGoodIn

_____

_____

_____

11

Successful businesses are often composed of happy employees, and successful leaders create and maintain a positive culture in order to achieve #BusinessSuccess. #InviteGoodIn

_____

_____

_____

12

#InvitingGoodIn your business can produce tangible results that will not only last short term but also help change people and businesses to be better for the long term. #BusinessSuccess

_____

_____

_____

13

Are you setting up your business to allow your managers and employees to invite good in or to edge good out? If you want #BusinessSuccess, set your business up to #InviteGoodIn!

_____

_____

_____

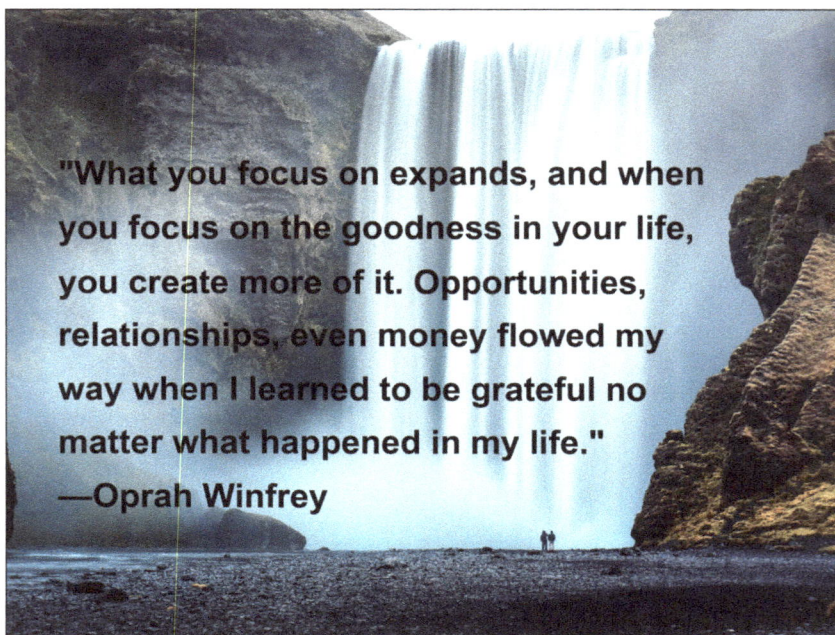

"What you focus on expands, and when you focus on the goodness in your life, you create more of it. Opportunities, relationships, even money flowed my way when I learned to be grateful no matter what happened in my life."
—Oprah Winfrey

Steve Rodgers
https://aha.pub/IGIPrinciples

At the very end of this section, share the AHA messages from this book socially by going to **https://aha.pub/IGIPrinciples**.

Section II

The Power of Gratitude

In business and in life, bad things can happen just as often as good things. Bad things often affect everyone. They can create fear, worry, and stress, which reduces the ability of people to work effectively and efficiently.

This section discusses the power of gratitude, and how it can create team collaboration that drives success. Some business owners and leaders may think that gratitude does not have much to do with success. However, it can produce a certain energy that brings about positivity and productivity that ultimately leads to success.

Negative situations happen both in our personal lives and in business. In life, there are tragedies such as disease, financial problems, death, etc. In business, there are unmet sales goals, unhappy customers, unproductive teams, and dissatisfied employees.

What one focuses their attention and energy on, grows. A business owner, or team leader, overly focusing on the negative things that the team is doing and neglecting to praise the positives, gives energy to negativity and causes it to grow. When leaders express gratitude and encouragement, the employees are inspired and supported to achieve their highest potential.

IGI-oriented leaders would benefit from making a conscious effort to find something to be grateful for despite negative situations. They can have faith that something good can come out of the situation. A culture and atmosphere of positivity in a business means that even seemingly negative situations can be turned into positive outcomes.

Imagine looking at the Google Earth app on a phone. It will first show a specific house, and then its neighborhood, and then its community. Zoom a little farther out, and it will show the country where this particular house is situated. Zoom out some more, and it will show the world—the green, blue, and round Earth in all its glory. That's what perspective looks like. When owners and leaders know how to focus on the big picture, rather than nitpick on the small, sometimes unnecessary happenings in the workplace, it's easier to be grateful. Often even finding solutions for any challenges they face. What some may consider to be obstacles, can actually be used as stepping stones to go to the next level.

The flow of gratitude begins at the very top of an organization and flows all the way to the very bottom. An owner or CEO who allows their employees to witness their gratitude is one who inspires loyalty and respect. This attitude of thankfulness is contagious and is felt by all who come into contact with the business.

When individuals don't find gratitude in negative situations, life can become scary and overwhelming. When they do have a gratitude mindset, they can make sense of the things happening to them. This helps prevent fear and create great calmness. Learning, healing, and growth come with the power of gratitude.

Business owners and other leaders also must inspire everyone in their business to have a gratitude mindset. This will result in interesting conversations. What happened within the team that they are grateful for? What has a team member done for another? Successful business leaders ask questions that can ignite the hearts of everyone on their team. They lead by example and create more gratitude within the business. In business settings, *Inviting Gratitude In*—another IGI principle—is essentially giving the space to allow that energy in the workplace.

Gratitude is the consciousness and openness to be grateful for someone, for something—anything!—at work. This can be practiced by sharing highlights from different teams: the things that have been accomplished successfully, the wins, the gains, profits, and the new projects and clients that came in, among others.

These kinds of conversations open up discussions, meetings, and dialogues for gratefulness, resulting in productivity, happiness, awareness, and appreciation of each other.

Business owners have the ability to allow everyone in the organization to find tangible expressions of gratitude. Have a poster board dedicated to praising great work, begin meetings with space for shout-outs for specific performance successes, dedicate a section of the website or company newsletter to recognizing excellence, engage in collective community service and charity projects, etc. There are an endless number of ways that gratitude can be taken from a silent feeling, and shared with all, so that everyone is encouraged and the flow of positivity is increased.

Another way that IGI-oriented leaders can create a culture of gratitude is by participating in charity work. This activity allows everyone to contribute to something bigger than themselves. Additionally, having a gratitude culture helps make everyone working in the business feel that they're in a place where serving others is far more important than the financials. If owners and leaders want to *Invite GOodness Into* their businesses, they must inspire gratitude in everyone working there.

Owners can even find gratitude in the challenges in their life and business. Often, life's greatest gifts come disguised as our worst nightmares. When challenges and struggles come to a company, it is life's way of showing how it needs to evolve and transform to meet this challenge. Rather than despairing and lashing out in frustration and anger, this is an opportunity to dig deeper within and find the inner resources to meet the challenge. If owners can say "thank you" to the universe for giving what they do not prefer, they then have the power to transform the situation into something that they do prefer.

The best owners and leaders understand that the power of gratitude greatly catapults a business to success. When they stay positive and are grateful for everything that happens, they become even better leaders. They will inspire others to always be grateful. When they allow and inspire gratitude within the business, the workplace becomes more vibrant.

Gratitude activates hard work. It comes full circle because when hard work pays off, people can't help but be grateful. Great learning, healing, and growth come with it. It's like pieces of a puzzle making more sense because leaders, owners, and the entire organization are filled with gratitude at seeing the big picture.

Gratitude is a natural phenomenon, and the highest form of gratitude is prayer. Gratitude and prayer is not so much an action but a state of being. To be living life in prayerfulness is to every moment be *Inviting GOodness In*. When in a state of gratitude, it is impossible to *Edge GOodness Out* because prayerfulness and gratitude are the opposite of ego.

Open hearts unlock gratitude. Gratitude makes people more human. It creates an energy of giving. It generates a collaborative environment. This is something that cannot be forced unless it is made a part of the experience in the organization by owners and leaders.

The quicker that everyone in the business gets into a gratitude mindset, the quicker they become happier and more productive, and the quicker the business can grow and succeed.

Scan the QR code or use this link to watch the section videos and more on this section topic:
https://steverodgers.net/the-power-of-gratitude

P.S. Don't forget to watch the videos at the end of each chapter. They will give you more direct perspective from the author. Also make sure you check out the links to the AHA Messages web page. You will find thousands more there from other amazing people on a very wide range of valuable topics!

14

There is a greater meaning and purpose for everything that is happening in your business. #FindGratitude and stay positive in order to drive more happiness and success in your life and in your business.

_____

_____

_____

15

There are two ways to look at life and the world. You can see the good or the bad. What we focus on and choose to see is what can bring us feelings of joy or feelings of despair. —Lloyd Newell via https://aha.pub/SteveRodgers #FindGratitude

_____

_____

_____

16

There are negative things that can happen within businesses: 1) unmet sales goals, 2) products fail, and 3) unhappy customers. Are you letting negative situations keep you from #FindingGratitude and fixing them?

_____

_____

_____

17

Great learning, healing, and growth are some of the results of #FindingGratitude for even the most tragic things that happened in your life and business.

_____

_____

_____

18

It takes no more time to see the good side of life than to see the bad. — Jimmy Buffett via https://aha.pub/SteveRodgers #FindGratitude

_____

_____

_____

19

Helping your managers and employees #FindGratitude when they're not grateful can bring about positivity in the workplace. Positive managers and employees are more effective, efficient, and successful.

_____

_____

_____

20

Showing #Gratitude toward managers and employees creates an energy of giving and collaboration that can help the business succeed. Are you spreading gratitude in your business?

_____

_____

_____

21

Open meetings by asking everyone what they are grateful for. Talking about gratitude opens up interesting dialogues within businesses that create more happiness, awareness, and success. #FindGratitude

_____

_____

_____

22

Businesses that do good things, in addition to their initial product or service, give their managers and employees something to be grateful for. Initiate a movement that they will want to be a part of and grateful for. #Gratitude

_____

_____

_____

23

Motivation for managers and employees often comes from being part of a business that allows them to contribute to something higher than themselves. #Gratitude #BusinessSuccess

_____

_____

_____

24

Track and measure how much your business is giving back and serving others. This allows everyone in your business to come together in #Gratitude and will drive #BusinessSuccess.

_____

_____

_____

25

The quicker you can be grateful for the negative things happening in your business, the lesser your fear is of not succeeding. Find the "good" in every situation. #FindGratitude

_____

_____

_____

26

To speak of gratitude is courteous and pleasant. To enact gratitude is generous and noble. But to live gratitude is to touch God. —Johannes Gaertner via https://aha.pub/SteveRodgers #FindGratitude

_____

_____

_____

27

Gratitude makes sense of our past, brings peace
for today, and creates a vision for tomorrow.
—Melody Beattie via https://aha.pub/SteveRodgers
#FindGratitude

_____

_____

_____

28

Train your mind to see the good in everything. Your
happiness and success in life and in business depends on
how you perceive the situations you're in. #FindGratitude

_____

_____

_____

"Forgiveness does not change the past, but it does enlarge the future." —Paul Boese

Steve Rodgers
https://aha.pub/IGIPrinciples

At the very end of this section, share the AHA messages from this book socially by going to **https://aha.pub/IGIPrinciples**.

Section III

The Power of Forgiveness

Many things happen within businesses and life—the good and the bad. Everyone in the business is human and has feelings. When employees are feeling down due to certain life or work situations, they often become unmotivated and unproductive. This can hinder business growth and success.

Business owners and leaders greatly benefit from understanding the importance of forgiveness in one's life. It allows people to free themselves from negativity. Having a culture of forgiveness can help drive more goodness, happiness, fulfillment, and success. The power of forgiveness gives room for people in businesses to fail, to be human, and to be vulnerable. Vulnerability is one of the things that can build trust within teams, and create a culture of teamwork and cooperation. When there is forgiveness, there is a commitment to change, show mercy, and not hold offense, so people can always stand up and try again when they fail.

Employees in an unforgiving company are so scared of making mistakes, that they also rarely have the confidence and security to take risks and obtain great successes. When they do make a mistake, they will hide it at all costs. This then creates an organization of secrecy, that has hundreds of small problems and mistakes hidden beneath the surface. A culture of forgiveness provides a space for everyone to do the right thing, knowing that nothing is unforgivable, and that honesty and transparency are always better in the long run.

It is a common problem in companies where petty personal disputes turn into grudges and grievances. This prevents harmonious teamwork, which in turn, hampers creativity and productivity. In providing an environment where coworkers can acknowledge their differences and find forgiveness, the company as a whole is strengthened.

To forgive is not to validate improper behavior. It is to acknowledge a mistake made in ignorance, error, or ego. Then allow the opportunity for everyone to move on and have another opportunity to succeed.

Forgiveness does not mean accepting or tolerating consistent behaviors that can harm you, the group, or the company. There may be unacceptable, or even criminal behavior, that may require serious actions to be taken. Situations such as HR issues that may require counseling or coaching, verbal or written warnings, and even possibly termination.

It doesn't mean these people have to stay in your environment to be forgiven. Sometimes it is time to forgive, and move someone out and onto their next career and life path. There is a saying, "You don't necessarily hire the wrong people, you sometimes keep the wrong people." This doesn't mean the people themselves are always wrong. It means that that person at this time is not right for their role, this team, or the company.

You can still accomplish the act and skill of forgiveness while setting healthy boundaries, expectations, and standards. Collectively this helps support a high-level work environment and company that all employees, and customers, can be proud of and drawn to, in their own various ways.

It takes a great deal of energy to remain in resentment and blame. It is much easier to show mercy, allow the past to remain in the past, and not be brought into the present. When someone refuses to forgive another, they are only harming themselves. Therefore, forgiveness is for our own benefit, as much as for the benefit of others.

For many individuals, it can be hard to encourage or even find forgiveness. To encourage is to add courage to another person, and to forgive, is to restore relationships by removing guilt, tension, or shame. Being unforgiving can affect one's professional or personal life. Many leaders hold their teams to high standards. However, dysfunctions often happen in the workplace. People have different personalities, backgrounds, and views, which can lead to massive dysfunction and politics. Within teams there can be backbiting, passive-aggressive behavior, competitiveness in dishonest ways, bullying, etc. All that can build up into resentment, competing factions, and failure in systems and performance. How can individuals deal with these imperfections?

IGI-oriented leaders who want to use the power of forgiveness to fuel their success can first understand that no business and no person is perfect. When an employee or a manager is found to be dishonest, forgiveness can be a hard choice to make, but it can be achieved without tolerating wrong attitudes and weak performances. Forgiveness does not mean forgetting the missteps and not correcting them. It means committing to do the right thing, and to make amends with people involved to maintain healthy relationships in the workplace. When leaders practice forgiveness, they inspire their respective teams to do the same: to be forgiving, to openly communicate regarding each other's differences, to strive to resolve conflicts amicably, to remain professional at all times, and to move forward in peace and with harmonious relationships.

Forgiveness can be manifested in times when owners or leaders have to make a decision that hurts, or goes against the expectations, of employees. They don't have to change the decisions they make, but they can apologize for how their decisions may have affected the employees. Forgiveness can bring trust, respect, dignity, grace, and humanity into the workplace. When changes are needed, on the other hand, business owners can maximize this opportunity to hear the concerns of the affected employees. They can encourage ideas and suggestions that will be

beneficial for the entire organization. In that way, forgiveness not only brings trust and respect, but also motivates the team to contribute to the initiatives and projects of the owners and leaders, so they know that they are valued members of the company.

Having forgiveness in one's heart and having the courage to seek it from others, can open up a path of energy that increases effectiveness and efficiency. This can be not only for one person but also for everyone around them. Forgiveness starts with leaders. They lead by example and inspire others in the business to live with forgiveness in their hearts, which leads to growth.

An owner or leader who has the humility to ask for the forgiveness of their employees for mistakes is one who teaches them that it is safe for them to be vulnerable and acknowledge their own mistakes. Rather than being a sign of weakness, this is a show of strength. Asking for forgiveness shows a willingness to improve, and do right by their employees, and the company as a whole.

Forgiveness is a hidden treasure. When entrepreneurs start to tap into it, a great power will be unleashed. It can open up a path of energy that improves performance and leads to a breakthrough. Just like with the famous quote, "With great power comes great responsibility," the power of forgiveness comes with the great ability to respond appropriately to different situations. In fact, this is not only useful in businesses, but it can also reflect in the personal lives of any individual.

For many, a lack of forgiveness is the only thing that is holding them back from moving on and going forward. Holding resentment is a heavy chain tying us back to our past, and to what we do not want, prefer, or need. We think that we are justified in carrying this chain around with us—but this is never the case.

Remaining in judgment of another is never a good place to be in. A person in that place remains in the energy of judgment, within their mind and heart. A wise man once said, "Judge not, lest ye be judged." When we judge another, we are really only judging ourselves. This is because ultimately, there are no others—only other versions of our self. In finally finding forgiveness of oneself and others in our life, we may find that this was the cutting of the one string holding us back from attaining our goals, and living the life we desire.

When people think of forgiveness, they often think that it can only happen between two individuals. However, the most important form of forgiveness is being able to have compassion and mercifulness for *ourselves*. It is only when one has been able to forgive oneself, that they are able to forgive another.

Everyone has done things that they now regret, experienced shame, and felt guilt. Individuals can find forgiveness for themselves in the understanding that to err is human, and there is no need to hold onto our guilt and shame. In pardoning ourselves, we surrender our self-loathing and are open to receive grace and healing. Once this is completed, it is easy to forgive others because we know that they are just as forgivable as we are.

As Mark Twain so poetically stated, "Forgiveness is the fragrance that the violet sheds on the heel that has crushed it." Forgiveness is an act of love, even for those who may have hurt you in ignorance or fear. And fear is the lowest form of ego.

Owners, leaders, employees, and everyone can benefit from having forgiveness in their hearts because they don't have to feel stuck with ill feelings toward another person (or remain bitter about a situation), which only stops them from moving forward. To not forgive, is to remain in chains. To forgive, however, is to break free and advance. The power of forgiveness is to advance to experience breakthroughs applicable to both business and life in general.

Scan the QR code or use this link to watch the section videos and more on this section topic:
https://steverodgers.net/the-power-of-forgiveness

29

Having a culture of #Forgiveness in the business opens up a path of energy for everyone that will increase their effectivity and efficiency.

_____

_____

_____

30

Successful businesses are those who have united managers and employees. A culture of #Forgiveness reduces friction within the business.

_____

_____

_____

31

Create a culture that allows #Forgiveness to enter into your business because it will reduce any tensions managers and employees have built that can cause friction within business.

_____

_____

_____

32

In many businesses, politics and backbiting happen just as much as teamwork and cooperation. What do you want more of in your business? If you want teamwork and cooperation, create a culture of #Forgiveness.

_____

_____

_____

33

Are you holding everyone in your business to very high standards and not accepting anything less than their best? Remember, they're human too. #Forgive them if they don't meet your expectations all the time.

_____

_____

_____

34

Allow people in your business the space to fail, to be human, and to be vulnerable. This often brings more happiness into the business, and that can drive success. #Forgiveness

_____

_____

_____

35

Humans are not perfect. Why would a business be perfect? #Forgiveness

_____

_____

_____

36

Allowing #Forgiveness within the business doesn't only mean forgiving people for not achieving their goals. It also means encouraging them to try again.

37

Forgiveness is not a feeling; it is a commitment.
It is a choice to show mercy and not hold offense.
Forgiveness is an expression of love.
—Gary Chapman via https://aha.pub/SteveRodgers

38

#Forgiveness gives you the power to break through unknown or unexpected walls that keep you from doing something good and creating more empowerment for your people.

_____

_____

_____

39

If you made a decision and a manager or employee felt bad because of it, ask for #Forgiveness
—not because of the decision you made, but because it hurt someone's feelings or morale.

_____

_____

_____

40

Just because you made a decision that hurt someone:
1) it doesn't mean that your decision wasn't the right
thing to do, and 2) it doesn't mean that you can't
apologize for how it affected someone and
still stay the decided course. #Forgiveness

_____

_____

_____

41

Asking for #Forgiveness doesn't mean you're apologizing
for a decision you made. It means you're acknowledging
that the people who were affected by the decision are
human and felt differently than you did.

_____

_____

_____

42

Asking for #Forgiveness, being forgiven, and forgiving others can give you more fulfillment and satisfaction as you strive toward success without feeling like a victim.

_____

_____

_____

43

Asking for #Forgiveness opens up a path for you to create a business that has managers and employees who do the right thing. Do you want to inspire everyone in your business to do the right thing?

_____

_____

_____

44

Are you vulnerable enough to ask for forgiveness or forgive someone else? Business owners and leaders who show vulnerability inspire everyone in the business to have #Forgiveness in their lives and be at peace.

_____

_____

_____

45

How much energy does it take when you try not to think of a person by not communicating? #Forgiveness allows you to free yourself from things that are keeping you from being productive and more empowered.

_____

_____

_____

46

What is success? It is being able to go to
bed each night with your soul at peace.
—Paulo Coelho via https://aha.pub/SteveRodgers
#Forgiveness

_____

_____

_____

47

The quicker you can get to #Forgiveness, the quicker you
can be more empowered to do good things. Try getting to
#Forgiveness in days versus weeks, months, or years.

_____

_____

_____

48

Are you feeling stuck and you can't get to the next level you want your business to be on? A culture of #Forgiveness in a business allows creativity and better performance to enter to get you to the next level.

_____

_____

_____

49

#Forgiveness is a hidden treasure. When you open it up, it unleashes great performance and power in your life and here in your business, and that can help drive success.

_____

_____

_____

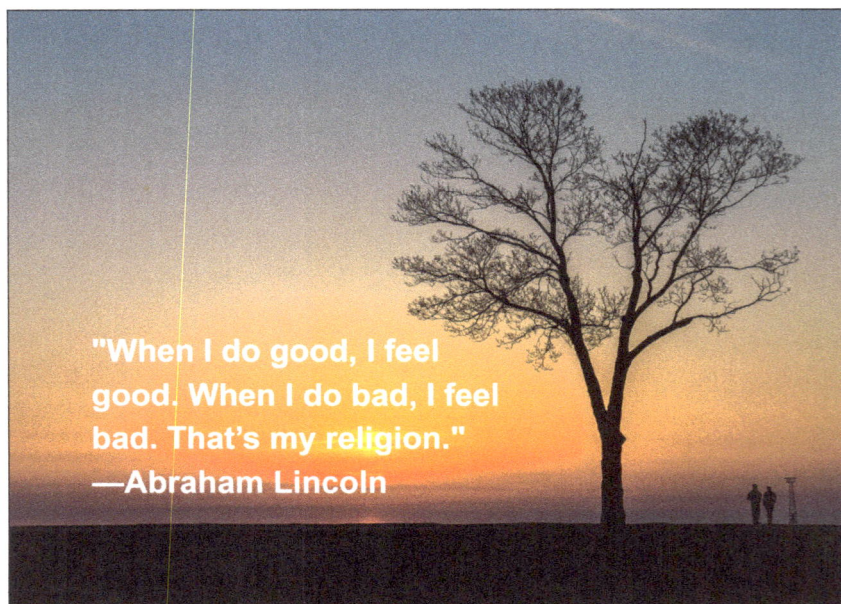

"When I do good, I feel good. When I do bad, I feel bad. That's my religion."
—Abraham Lincoln

Steve Rodgers
https://aha.pub/IGIPrinciples

At the very end of this section, share the AHA messages from this book socially by going to **https://aha.pub/IGIPrinciples**.

Section IV

Living Up to Your Moral Fiber and Choosing to Do the Right Thing

All humans have their own moral fiber and have free will. Everyone has the power to choose whether they will live up to their morals, and how they deal with what happens in their lives.

True empowerment is knowing that a business owner can be as successful as they desire to be, without having to hurt anyone or anything else to achieve this. The old ideas that businesses need to push the lines and possibly operate unethically in order to get a leg up on the competition are no longer acceptable. These times demand that businesses act in even higher levels of integrity, which is important for every leader or entrepreneur. Having integrity in and out of the workplace is to be integrated—for all aspects of oneself and one's actions need to be in harmony and congruent with each other. Without it, others quickly learn that they cannot trust their leader. Sooner or later, a person acting out of integrity will see their incongruous actions returning to them, creating chaos and suffering for themselves and others.

The existential threat of climate destruction and the increasingly obvious injustices in our society mean that a conscious, activist mindset is no longer only a fringe value. If individuals don't take action in their lives to ensure that their actions serve to better humanity and the Earth, then they are only contributing to more suffering and injustice in the world.

The owner of the business sets the tone for how successful they want their businesses to be. They are responsible for everything that happens. Responsibility is simply the ability to respond to what the situation requires. If an individual does not take responsibility for anything, then they do not have agency and cannot change the situation. An owner must take responsibility for everything about their business and how it impacts the world, as they create a culture where everyone does the right thing at all times. This can drive a great deal of goodness, happiness, and success.

This section talks about three important steps that IGI-oriented leaders can take in order to *Invite GOodness In*-to their lives and businesses. The first step is to define their moral fiber: What matters most to them? What do they value? The next step is to determine how they can live up to their moral fiber in both their professional and personal lives. Finally, they must see if their actions are aligned with their moral fiber.

To live up to one's moral fiber, is to stand up for everything one truly believes in. It's also about taking full responsibility to live that way every day. Moral fiber can get lost when conflict arises, employees make mistakes, or the business encounters challenges that require actions that go against one's values. That is why managers must track their decisions and actions.

Business leaders must walk the talk. Their decisions must be according to the tenets of their moral fiber, such as by consistently acting on the mission of their businesses and their vision statements. When someone in the company takes an action that is against one or two of the tenets of their moral fiber, what will they do? Will they tolerate it? Setting a good example as an owner and leader always goes a long way in any organization.

Many employees (even clients) look at how owners and executives are consistent with what they say and what they do, which results in loyalty and cooperation (and repeat business with clients). This is where honesty and integrity come in. As leaders, the choices they make are born out of their own free will. Nobody forces anything on them. Every decision, every action (or reaction), is ultimately driven by what's true to their hearts and intentions. That can give peace in the decisions we make.

Generally, someone's happiness level is based on how they choose responsibility for everything they do. What's visible in their life is what they choose to be transparent with to show that they are accountable for their own actions. It's the same for owners and leaders in their circle of influence. For every single thing that happens in their lives, whether it be good, tragic, bad, humorous, or ugly, there is zero-tolerance for victim mentality. One must assume responsibility for every decision they make. Just because someone did not give them a break, or they were met by a great tragedy, does not mean that they no longer have a choice. Although certain things in their lives worked in the past and certain things didn't, these all add up to help them better improve the way they are today. Every single person has a choice, and responsibility, to act and move forward to be successful.

When leaders make a decision to uphold their moral fiber, it must be done while considering the consequences. They must understand the immediate impact and all the ripple effects in the future, as well as the possible bottom line. The right thing still must be done, no matter how unpopular or difficult it may be.

IGI-oriented leaders can lead by example, when demonstrating that they will not tolerate certain things that go against their moral fiber. Providing examples helps everyone in the company to understand that, they too, have the power to do what they think is right. Owners and leaders can then expect and demand that others take equal, and swift, action on events that could destroy the values of the business. Free will is a human right. It applies to any religious thinking, the hierarchy of education, and even the corporate setting. Owners have small and large decisions to make every single day and they learn very quickly there are consequences for every choice the make, so they must choose wisely.

It's important that owners and leaders refrain from forcing such decisions, but rather develop effective communication strategies to deliver the message behind their actions, this will help gain adoption much faster.

IGI-aligned leaders have the opportunity to make every decision a learning and humbling moment. That leads others to have the courage to take the same path—the path of living up to one's personal moral fiber and that of the business, no matter what it takes. When in charge a leader needs to take charge, do the right thing, and always take the high road.

When pursuing the right thing, it is expected that IGI-oriented leaders will rock the boat, because others will be faced with doing something that they have never done before. It is important to take bold actions, state their intention of what's needed to be done, what they're willing to do to make that happen, and commit to actually making it work. Taking risks, making difficult choices, and delivering results are all part of the journey. The only way to grow is to advance by taking responsibility especially in the very toughest of situations..

Scan the QR code or use this link to watch the section videos and more on this section topic:
https://steverodgers.net/living-up-to-your-moral-fiber-and-choosing-to-do-the-right-thing

50

All humans have the freedom to choose what happens in their lives. Living up to your moral fiber and choosing to #DoTheRightThing can help you achieve #BusinessSuccess and happiness.

_____

_____

_____

51

Your happiness level in your life and business is based on: 1) how much you choose to take responsibility for everything that is happening, and 2) how much you choose to #DoTheRightThing.

_____

_____

_____

52

Understanding that you are responsible for everything
that happens in your life and in your business creates:
1) more happiness and fulfillment and
2) less stress and fear. #DoTheRightThing

_____

_____

_____

53

How we look at any situation and how we view the world
is always our own choice. We have the power to choose
what we can do to make a difference in each moment, in
each situation, and in each day. #DoTheRightThing

_____

_____

_____

54

Moral fiber is the quality of being determined to do what one thinks is good. Success in life and in business often comes to those who are determined to #DoTheRightThing.

_____

_____

_____

55

Define your moral fiber and live it on a daily, weekly, and monthly basis. When you live up to your moral fiber and #DoTheRightThing, you invite goodness into your life and into your business.

_____

_____

_____

56

Responsibility is accepting that you are the cause and the solution of a matter. It's up to you to determine what your next step is. #DoTheRightThing

_____

_____

_____

57

Successful business owners and leaders know that they are responsible for speaking up and taking action when things such as racism, sexism, or bullying happen within the business. #DoTheRightThing

_____

_____

_____

58

Take a stance when things are happening in your business that are not part of your moral fiber. #DoTheRightThing

_____

_____

_____

59

When placed in command, take charge. Always take the high road, always, and #DoTheRightThing to achieve #BusinessSuccess.

_____

_____

_____

60

Your decisions are significant. They don't only affect you. They affect others and ripple out to the rest of the world. Are you deciding for the greater good? #DoTheRightThing

_____

_____

_____

61

Before making a decision, think about how it can affect others in the business. Doing so allows you to make better decisions that can help the business succeed. #DoTheRightThing

---

62

Communicating the choices you're making and your intentions with others in the business can inspire them to do the same and support you. #DoTheRightThing

---

63

Successful business owners and leaders who make decisions that live up to their moral fiber set an example for their managers and employees to do the same in their own space within the business. #DoTheRightThing

_____

_____

_____

64

Collective consciousness is when everyone in your business is aware that they have the right to speak up about their situations, whether good or bad. Allow them to be whole individuals within the business vs. being in an isolated bubble.

_____

_____

65

Are you creating collective consciousness in your business? Collective consciousness helps drive business owners, leaders, and their managers and employees to do good for each other and to others outside the business.

_____

_____

_____

66

Managers and employees who are aware that their choices affect others besides themselves often become more engaged and motivated to better the business. Are you creating this awareness in your business? #DoTheRightThing

_____

_____

_____

67

Managers and employees who have the mindset that: 1) they are the CEO of their surrounding environment and 2) their choices affect everyone, often choose to #DoTheRightThing. Inspire your managers and employees to do the right thing!

_____

_____

68

Leadership is all about people—not organizations, not plans, and not strategies. It is about people motivating people to do good things. —Colin Powell via https://aha.pub/SteveRodgers #DoTheRightThing

_____

_____

_____

69

Allow your managers and employees to take action and #DoTheRightThing when they see that there's something happening in the business that's not aligned with their moral compass.

_____

_____

_____

70

Everything that happens in the business happens for a reason. Conscious business owners and leaders understand that they get to choose what happens next. #DoTheRightThing

_____

_____

_____

71

In difficult situations, do you let negatives persist and cause problems, or do you take action and fix them? #DoTheRightThing #BusinessSuccess

_____

_____

_____

72

When you feel stuck, realize that you may be staying stuck for a reason. Is it because you weren't ready to take the next step? You have a choice: Do you stay stuck or do you take action? #DoTheRightThing

_____

_____

_____

73

Successful business owners, leaders, and employees don't wait for someone to decide what their paths look like. They confidently choose to #DoTheRightThing and take action. #BusinessSuccess

_____

_____

_____

74

The time is always right to do what is right.
—Martin Luther King Jr.
via https://aha.pub/SteveRodgers #DoTheRightThing

_____

_____

_____

75

You have a choice to #DoTheRightThing. Follow your
instinct, follow your gut, and be the person you really
want and need to be. #BusinessSuccess

_____

_____

_____

76

We shape the results of our efforts according to our choices along the way. #DoTheRightThing

_____

_____

_____

77

Whatever your dream is, it is out there and it is possible
if you choose to do what it takes to make it real.
#DoTheRightThing

_____

_____

_____

78

All positive and negative things that happen to you in the
present allow you to see positive things in the future.
Choose to #DoTheRightThing today to see a positive
future tomorrow. #BusinessSuccess

_____

_____

_____

"When you learn, teach.
When you get, give."
—Maya Angelou

Steve Rodgers
https://aha.pub/IGIPrinciples

At the very end of this section, share the AHA messages from this book socially by going to **https://aha.pub/IGIPrinciples**.

Section V

The Power of Being of Service and Paying It Forward

Many business owners and CEOs who have reached the top of the ladder often feel lonely. Even after achieving massive success, they feel like maybe there is still something missing. Fabricated titles and a high paycheck are just not always enough, despite how great they may seem. What is the reason for this? Why does it seem to be not enough? What could be missing?

More and more people are seeking to express their deepest purpose in their professional lives, and eliminate the separation between their inner and outer lives—their life and their work. Without understanding and acting on their soul's purpose, individuals feel unfulfilled, and their work in the world is less potent than it is professed, or meant to be. Everyone deep down desires a way to do well and to do good, and to do well by doing good.

This section is about servant leadership and how it can create truly satisfying success. Servant leadership is another level on the ladder of success. It means being of service and truly caring about other people. Servant leadership is not expecting anything in return but having the pure intention to serve others.

Personal success and service to others—are these two desires compatible? Is it possible to achieve one's dreams in business and not only do no harm but also be a force of good in the world?

Central to this is understanding that one does not have to choose between service to self and service to others. A higher understanding knows that self and others are one. Therefore, service to others is service to self, and service to self is service to others. What we are doing is service to all.

Being of service to all implies that entrepreneurs understand that there is more to life than making profits and material gain. They would benefit to understand that they exist on this Earth to do their part in building a better world that everyone knows is possible. That they contribute their unique piece of the puzzle.

IGI-oriented leaders can realize the value of servant leadership. However, some see it as a weakness. On the contrary, servant leadership is a very big and deep strength. Some executives feel that they are not at the top of the ladder to serve but to be served. Owners and leaders who only think of themselves *Edge GOodness Out* of their lives and their businesses. This can lead to unhappy employees, dissatisfied customers, and lost opportunities. It can also lead to an unsatisfied personal life.

Unlike titles and paychecks, servant leadership can bring unlimited and sustainable benefits. If individuals want to invite more goodness into their lives and their businesses, they would benefit from adopting a servant leadership mindset and start paying it forward.

Individuals can be of service to others in big or small ways. They can anticipate what others need. They can create a miracle in somebody else's life just by helping out.

It is an old, outdated, and false idea that the way to succeed in business is to get ahead at all costs, and to care nothing for the greater good. The world is rapidly changing, and there is no longer any place for financial success without moral integrity. In the past, these two things could be mutually exclusive. However, today, businesses and individuals must "do good" to "do well."

People are seeking to do business with and buy products from organizations that are conscious, and acting in integrity, in all aspects of their operation—whether that be how they treat their employees, their impact on the environment, and the overall consciousness of the business.

The old paradigm believed that one had to choose either financial success or helping others, and that one could not accomplish both. The business leaders of today and tomorrow understand that one does not have to choose between these two, but that the more one helps others, the more personal success they and their business receive.

To do well is to do good, and to do good is to do well. These two are one and the same.

This becomes an ever-increasing flow of benefit for both, which mutually magnifies the good that a business owner can do in the world, and the amount of financial success that they attain.

Being of service invites more goodness, which in turn, drives more success. This turns into a powerful, ever-growing force of positive energy, that permeates the entire company, from the management to employees and customers. Everyone feels good about what they are doing and so has more energy and enthusiasm. The new paradigm is one of universal abundance and cooperation, rather than the old false beliefs in scarcity and lack. The truth is that there are more than enough resources for everyone on the planet to live in luxury, so there is no need to attempt to get ahead by trampling others on the way to the top. Being of service magnifies the axiom of "doing well by doing good." Great things can happen to you when you help others first. Owners and leaders who do good things for others receive goodness back in one way or another, encouraging others to do good things as well. Being of service is noble work. Not only does it add value to the servant leader, but it also adds value to the people served, because of the high honor that comes with just being around anyone or anything that involves serving others. Anticipating what others need is a high-quality trait of any leader. Being of service also creates value, such as in activities like volunteering, giving back to causes, etc.

It is a law of life that everything a person creates returns to them. In serving others through a business, the fruits of the work benefit others, which in turn, rebound upon the entrepreneur. They don't need to choose between these two seemingly contradictory values—they can shift their mindset so they can see how these are actually the same thing. The way to make money is to help others make money, and to be successful is to provide others the opportunity for success. By serving both others and oneself, owners benefit while achieving their personal dreams and goals.

One becomes rich by making others rich, and not just financially. Ask yourself: How can I help myself and others become rich in all ways? In relationships, mental/emotional life, spirituality, and finances?

Being of service leads to stronger connections with teams and clients. It also opens opportunities for them to be seen as vulnerable. When managers show vulnerability through a servant leadership mindset, everyone will voluntarily follow and support them. Teams and employees will start improving in their work because they want to, not because they have to.

Employees are motivated by being part of a company that allows them to contribute to something higher than themselves. If they feel that they are contributing to a better world, their actions are inspired and effortless, as they flow from love and joy. By supporting and encouraging employees to feel that each day they are doing a service for the world, they will be both more productive and happier. This good energy then permeates the entire business and is felt by all who come into contact with it.

Mentorships and coaching models are vital aspects of servant leadership. When leaders do one-on-ones, it shows accountability and creates more value and opportunities for the employees and for the whole team. This leads to better connections and work relationships because owners and leaders can evaluate the reason for doing what they're doing and not just entirely focusing on the results they hope to achieve. Results such as gaining more revenue and getting profit from meeting sales targets. Servant leaders are not afraid to be vulnerable to show their authentic selves. When leaders are strong enough to be vulnerable, the number of people who follow them and do things for them increases.

Beyond the money that entrepreneurs aspire to make, the opportunity to serve others will allow them to extend grace and blessings to others. They can then be conduits and distribution centers of goodwill, and to contribute to something higher than themselves. This is where management can organize charities, or partner with non-profit organizations, to provide basic needs to communities for a good cause. Giving back to such communities is as important as earning revenue, hitting performance metrics, and acquiring new accounts.

There is a higher and greater reward for those who serve others. Being of service invites more goodness, which in turn, drives more success. When owners and leaders build businesses that are of service to each other and then pay it forward, employees are more motivated and engaged to do good things.

Being of service and paying it forward starts with the leaders of an organization. When employees see that their leaders are doing good things for others, they develop the same mindset. If everybody is being of service and paying it forward, they all help the business and everyone around them be more successful.

Scan the QR code or use this link to watch the section videos and more on this section topic:
https://steverodgers.net/the-power-of-being-of-service-and-paying-it-forward

79

Being of service and paying it forward magnifies God or goodness in your business. The more your business is serving others, the more people are driven to help the business succeed.

_____

_____

_____

80

There's not much fulfilment in just making more money or getting more titles. If you want fulfilment plus the money and the titles, #BeOfService. #BusinessSuccess

_____

_____

_____

81

Do you want to achieve truly fulfilling #BusinessSuccess? #BeingOfService can provide you with unlimited and sustainable fulfillment while just obtaining profits and a cool title won't.

_____

_____

_____

82

The way you view serving customers matters. Businesses that believe that #BeingOfService is one of the most important jobs in the world are often those that achieve #BusinessSuccess.

_____

_____

_____

83

Many successful businesses:
1) anticipate what their managers, employees, and customers need before they know they need it, and
2) help them satisfy those needs. #BeOfService

_____

_____

_____

84

Businesses can achieve lucrative opportunities and money by #BeingOfService and creating value that people are willing to pay for. #BusinessSuccess

_____

_____

_____

85

When you create value by #BeingOfService to your customers, they understand why they should do business with you instead of someone else. #BusinessSuccess

_____

_____

_____

86

Businesses that are serving others accomplish two things: 1) they create better relationships and 2) they achieve higher profits. Do you want to create fruitful relationships with your managers, employees, and customers? #BeOfService #BusinessSuccess

_____

_____

_____

87

Having a servant leadership mindset creates joy, peace, and fulfilment in one's role in the business. Do you want a business that has happy and fulfilled managers and employees? Inspire them to #BeOfService and #PayItForward.

88

When you do a good deed, show what that good deed did for others and the business. Sharing goodness often motivates someone else in the business to do good too and then it spreads to others. #PayItForward

---

89

IGI-oriented business owners and leaders inspire their employees to #BeOfService to others. This drives managers and employees to work because they want to, not because they have to.

_____

_____

_____

90

Getting other people to #PayItForward and do good things can help ignite more goodness in the world. What can you or your business do to help someone else have the same mindset?

_____

_____

_____

91

Don't wait until you get to a level of abundance and prosperity and for a long stretch of time before giving back and #PayingItForward. You can make a difference in someone else's life now!

_____

_____

_____

92

When you #PayItForward, you just do it without expecting anything in return. You have already gotten all that you were supposed to receive because someone else probably paid it forward to you.

_____

_____

_____

93

Life is good! How do you #PayItForward?
—Marshall Goldsmith via https://aha.pub/SteveRodgers

_____

_____

_____

94

Businesses who are #BeingOfService and
#PayingItForward create miracles for those they touch,
and inspire others to want to do business with them.

_____

_____

_____

Let go into the mystery
Let yourself go
You've got to open up your heart
That's all I know
Trust what I say and do what you're told
Baby, and all your dirt will turn into gold
— Van Morrison

Steve Rodgers
https://aha.pub/IGIPrinciples

At the very end of this section, share the AHA messages from this book socially by going to **https://aha.pub/IGIPrinciples**.

Section VI

Letting Go and Turning Things Over to Trust

Most business owners and leaders are used to having control over everyone and everything in their businesses, but the reality is that no one can have full control of everything in their life. There are times when all one can do is just let go, trust, and let things unfold on their own.

IGI-oriented leaders can understand that sometimes a higher power has something amazing in store for them. Letting go of control and trusting that higher power can help guide them to where they want to be in their life and business— and it's often better than they ever expected. Veering away from planned steps can be good, because when individuals follow their gut instinct that tells them to go in another direction, it can actually lead to good things.

This section discusses how letting go of control can be a good choice. No matter how hard entrepreneurs try to achieve an outcome, things will not always go their way. Once they know what they want to accomplish and have done what they need to do, they just have to trust that a higher power will help them be successful.

Leaders sometimes have the tendency to take too much control, which could lead to shutting off ideas or people. It's important to remind them that they don't need to be the driver at all times—they can have as much fun in the passenger seat. This entails delegating tasks and collaborating more to encourage employees to step up and add their supply of skills and talent for tasks at hand. The results will be two-fold: (1) employees gain the confidence to take on leadership roles because they know the management trusts them, and (2) the organization achieves more because more heads are working together.

As the CEO of a company or whatever their role and title is, individuals can always remember that they are the CEO of their own destiny, their own life, and their own environment. Therefore, they can make an impact on the people around them, driving revenue, providing excellent customer service, making smart and level-headed decisions, managing work and life commitment, exemplifying integrity, etc. This does not mean that they are supposed to manage the lives of other people in the same organization. The synergy in the team—building trust, vulnerability, integrity, and cooperation—is what makes teams work.

Promotions can also come faster, as people will rise up to meet the tasks delegated to them. One of the biggest disservices in the workplace industry is when employers don't provide a good environment for the employees to learn, grow, and rise to the next level with appropriate compensation and benefits. On the employee's side, the disservice is in being less enthused and doing work that they are not passionate about, as they are just there for the paycheck, with no career plans or growth pattern whatsoever.

Owners and leaders are best served by following their gut, which sometimes requires doing something without being sure how it will turn out. If things don't work out as planned, there may be another way to get there. When business leaders let go of control, life can become a dance of romance, and not a pressure-filled journey to success. They are more open to ideas from others.

When setting plans and budgets, business leaders have to deal with numbers and people. How much is the marketing budget? What's the projection for this quarter? What's the new product offering? How many people are going to buy it? In all these decision-making processes, they need to tell their team the end result to achieve and ask for any ideas.

Having space where everyone in the business is allowed to express their ideas can open opportunities for growth. It creates freedom of expression, which can lead to free-flowing channels of creativity that can take the business to a new level.

Even if ideas suggested by team members fail, they will be even more motivated to keep them coming until the desired outcome is reached. Letting them pursue their gut feeling, giving it a chance to grow, and tracking its result can create new and wonderful things in the business. That's how new ideas are born every day.

When owners and leaders run their business without trying to take full control over it, their job and their life feel lighter. They must realize that everything happening in their lives and businesses has value and meaning. There are amazing things that can come from giving up the steering wheel and leaving it to trust. IGI-oriented entrepreneurs are brave enough to surrender control to those who work for them, as well as the higher spiritual intelligence in charge of their life.

There comes a time in a person's life when they come to understand that along with hard work and the attempt to realize their goals, they must also learn to surrender their personal will. Doing so opens themselves to an intelligence that transcends their own. Sometimes trusting what you cannot see is hard and even undesired. However, I have found that trusting in a power greater than myself, which I choose to call God, allows my faith muscle to be exercised and strengthened every day. The more I practice trust, the more my trust is rewarded, which generates more ability to trust in an ongoing, deepening cycle.

We must realize that life is a process, that it takes time and consistent effort to produce anything of value and see the results. Usually, we have to set our ego aside as best we can, dig deep into our unseen energy, and draw on our inner resources. We then can simply take consistent action for days, weeks, months, or even years to move forward or evolve. We are better served by accepting ourselves and our situation as it is, while also taking steps each day to get where we desire to be.

Once you accept this process and surrender to anything you struggle to initiate - be it eating a healthier diet, starting a workout plan, training to run a marathon, writing a book, or working toward any other goal - changes will happen. There is a magic that occurs when we accept our situation and surrender to the process without insistence on a particular outcome. Simultaneously, while being crystal clear as to what we want, and what we don't want. Then, when you add in the secret sauce of the "why" and tap into that at the root level, you have a strong foundation and the fuel to achieve great things.

Many see surrender as a giving up of one's power. However, surrender is not the giving up of power, but surrendering to the power that one already has, and always contains, but didn't even realize. We may experience the source of our power to be outside of ourselves temporarily until we change our perspective. Similar to the analogy I shared earlier about dipping an empty glass into the ocean and then returning it back to the ocean. Even though it was temporarily separated from its source, it was still always a part of the entire ocean. By *Inviting GOodness In*, one surrenders their false, pseudo-power, for their true power. They tap into their true power when they allow themselves to follow their heart and be in service to the whole, rather than a selfish, separate self.

People who do this may find that things magically fall into place, better than they could ever have imagined. When our expectations are relaxed and insistence upon a particular outcome is let go, something better than one's wildest imaginings can manifest. The fact is that nobody knows what the best possible outcome is, and relinquishing the white-knuckled grip upon what happens in our lives can naturally, and spontaneously, provide us with exactly what we need.

By moving from ego to IGI, entrepreneurs learn that by *Inviting GOod In* they gain more than they could ever possibly have by acting alone. They surrender their egoic separate self and open themselves to being supported and inspired by a force that is infinitely more wise and powerful than their limited, thinking self.

Scan the QR code or use this link to watch the section videos and more on this section topic:
https://steverodgers.net/letting-go-and-turning-things-over-to-trust

"P.S. Don't forget to watch the videos at the end of each chapter. They will give you more direct perspective from the author. Also make sure you check out the links to the AHA Messages web page. You will find thousands more there from other amazing people on a very wide range of valuable topics!"

95

God (or a higher power) communicates in different ways (e.g., premonitions or instincts). Open yourself up and #Trust that a higher power will guide you toward happiness and #BusinessSuccess.

_____

_____

_____

96

Many business owners and leaders are used to having control, even though they're not always in control. There will be times when we can relax and #Trust that God (or a higher power) is taking control for the better.

_____

_____

_____

97

Follow your instincts. Instincts can be signs given by a higher power that urge you to let go and #Trust that what's happening in your life or in your business is how it should be.

_____

_____

_____

98

If you want to achieve greater and lasting #BusinessSuccess, start conversations that allow space for God (or goodness) to enter and be revealed, and then pursued and expanded. #Trust

_____

_____

_____

99

Ask questions of everyone in your business that will allow #Trust conversations to be held in the boardroom. That allows people to have freedom of expression, creativity, and responsibility.

_____

_____

_____

100

Questions business owners and leaders can ask in order to allow #Trust in the business: 1) what's your gut telling you? or 2) do you have something that you believe is a little out of the ordinary but might have good results?

_____

_____

_____

101

New ideas are born from work environments that allow people in the business to express their feelings and beliefs, and let them pursue their gut. Are you setting your business up to allow new ideas to be born? #Trust #BusinessSuccess

---

102

Sometimes, when you turn things over to trust, it may not be aligned with what your initial plan was. #Trust that the direction you're going is just another path that will take you to your destination.

103

#Trust that there may be another way toward #BusinessSuccess, even if it takes longer and may even be completely different than what you originally thought.

_____

_____

_____

104

Accept what is, let go of what was,
and have faith in what will be.
—Sonia Ricotti via https://aha.pub/SteveRodgers #Trust

_____

_____

_____

105

There are amazing things that can come from giving up the steering wheel in your life and in your business, and leaving it to #Trust. Are you brave enough to do so? #BusinessSuccess

_____

_____

_____

106

You don't have to drive a car to enjoy the journey. Sometimes, just being in the passenger's seat and letting a higher power drive the car for you is very enjoyable and can help you achieve happiness and #BusinessSuccess. #Trust

_____

_____

_____

107

You don't have to know all the answers to your life right now. They will reveal themselves as you follow the path you're taking, step by step. Just be present in the moment and have #Trust.

_____

_____

_____

108

#Trust is taking the first step even when you don't see the whole staircase. You act with faith that a higher power will guide you on your journey toward success.

_____

_____

_____

109

When you want something, all the universe conspires in helping you to achieve it. —Paulo Coelho via https://aha.pub/SteveRodgers #Trust #BusinessSuccess

_____

_____

_____

110

Everything happens for a reason. #Trust that a higher power out there is guiding you to the best path that will lead to your happiness and your business's success.

_____

_____

_____

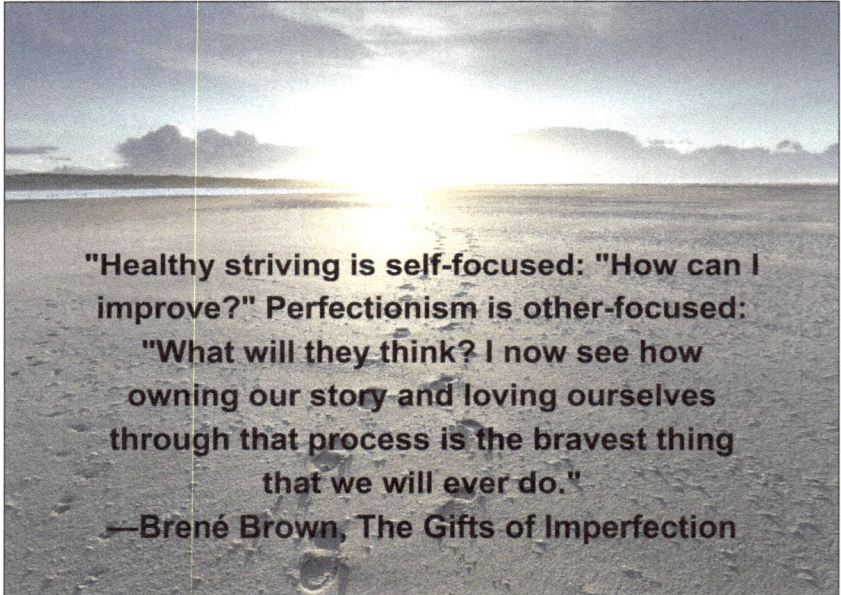

"Healthy striving is self-focused: "How can I improve?" Perfectionism is other-focused: "What will they think? I now see how owning our story and loving ourselves through that process is the bravest thing that we will ever do."
—Brené Brown, The Gifts of Imperfection

Steve Rodgers
https://aha.pub/IGIPrinciples

At the very end of this section, share the AHA messages from this book socially by going to **https://aha.pub/IGIPrinciples**.

Section VII

The Power of Daily Inventory and Course Correction — The 4 B's

Many business owners and leaders measure and track their sales, retention, and customer satisfaction to make sure their businesses are running well. The same can also be said for their daily lives. IGI-oriented leaders also would benefit from measuring and tracking the good things they do. Are there things they could be doing but aren't? Can there be improvements?

This section discusses the four most important things in a person's life and how important it is to have daily inventory and course correction.

Important things in one's life that need care are the 4 B's: *body*, *being*, *bonds*, and *business*. Everyone can benefit from making sure that they're taking care of these things on a daily basis. Doing so can help open up more goodness in life, as well as drive more balance, happiness, and success.

In order for individuals to measure and track their 4 B's, they would need to have a daily scorecard for displaying each one. These can be tracked and measured daily on a very easy looking tic-tac-toe score board. I have been using this system for years and it is very effective. You can view more about this topic in the section video. Setting goals to achieve and tracking what they're doing to achieve those goals can help keep everything measured, tracked, and in check. The goal is to get to 4 points a day or as close to 28 points a week as you can. Then you seek to steadily improve and try to get there in less time in the day. This is where true mastery comes into play.

The healthier and more energetic the physical body is, the more energy and vitality it has to put toward achieving one's career goals. It is not a luxury to care for the body, it is a necessity.

For the 1st B of the *body*, individuals can set goals such as eating healthy and routinely exercising. When they eat junk food or forget to exercise, they note that down on the scorecard. Keeping track of how much they're taking care of their body can help them achieve good health. For example, I am a vegan... I know, kinda crazy! I was a kid who was brought up on meat and potatoes, who could eat a pizza full of meat and cheese a few times a week. Also, at one point, I weighed over 300 pounds! But focusing month after month, year after year, I evolved to this new lifestyle. So, on my scorecard I get 1/2 point for eating healthy that day, and another 1/2 point for my daily exercise.

Entrepreneurs most likely also have religious or spiritual beliefs. They can measure and track this aspect of *being* as well, such as how often they pray or meditate, or when they go to their place of worship. There are many other ways one can do spiritual readings or practice their faith in daily life; walking around regularly in mother nature and communing with higher energies. If they fail to pray or meditate daily, that is something they can improve upon. If they have not spent enough time to meet with spiritual friends and family, to fellowship, share testimonies and life stories, that is something that can be tracked for improvement.

There are many ways that people can nurture their being. Find two key items that you value and add 1/2 point to each for a total of 1 point in the *being* category each day. I recommend you do something that focuses on fostering your own internal spiritual beliefs, like one of the suggested listed items, and then one that expresses your *being* essence in the world. This would be an act of kindness or positive action that has a spiritual level of impact in some way. By accomplishing these two daily tasks, you earn your full point in the category. If one is not drawn to meditation, yoga, or traditional spiritual practices, they can still strengthen their spiritual intelligence and connection to a higher power through any activity that engages their creativity. These can be activities that put them in nature and connects them with other beings. Perhaps hiking in the forest is their meditation, playing guitar is their prayer, or volunteering to help those in need is their yoga.

All people have and need human connections. *Bonds* is the 3rd B, it consists of family, friends, your romantic partner, peers, and new daily encounters with others. Relationships should be given as much time as monitoring the P&L and the balance sheet in their business. All work without socializing on a consistent basis, in ways that you enjoy, can take a toll on someone's body, mind, and soul. Bonds heal a person's soul. To be connected relationally with someone on a level, other than a work relationship, is essential to any individual, not limited to just owners and executives. This is something we all need. After all, we are not actually human beings, we are a spiritual being having a human experience. How can we explore more of what that journey of experience means for us in our relationship with other beings?

Life is a relationship. To exist is to be in relationship with all of creation. Everyone is in relationship with themselves, with their Creator, with other human beings, and with all of life. Here in the *bonds* scoring area, focus on action or behaviors that score you 1/2 point for a daily effort of improving a relationship inside your inner circle. But also have a daily practice of cultivating better and deeper relationships outside your inner circle. It can be a spontaneous kind text to a coworker, a private message to someone on social media about a good quality they may possess, or even simply making a special call or hand written note to someone in your outer circle. These acts may better someone's day, mindset, or psyche. We all want and need to be appreciated, and to know we matter, and that someone sees us and cares! Relationships serve as mirrors that reflect the truth to us. Without these mirrors, individuals would not receive feedback that is essential to become more of their true selves. Experiencing challenges in our relationships with others is a great opportunity for individuals to look within, and see what patterns of behavior they are engaging in that are creating this conflict, so as to heal.

IGI-oriented leaders must make sure they're working both on and in their businesses. *Business* is the 4th of the 4 B's. Many think that they're giving their best in the business by staying above the daily grind we all experience by replying to emails, returning calls or texts, and holding meetings. In other words, seeing to the running of the day-to-day business. What would benefit them potentially even more is to consciously "work on their business." That means working on marketing plans, prospecting, bettering employee and customer relationships, and bettering their own or their company's value proposition.

There are many areas to improve on for owners and executives in this aspect. Busyness is not equivalent to productivity. Ticking off to-do lists and checkboxes of tasks for the day aren't all that needs to be done for the business to run, nor is it fulfilling to do this day in and day out. Monthly and daily schedules, promotions, incentives, compensation and benefits, and 360 surveys to find answers to their employees' questions or how the leaders and managers are viewed and perceived—these are all important items that can be worked on to consistently grow the company. This is truly where EQ, IQ, personalities, and spiritual intelligence diverge. These are not always as tangible but are equally valuable assets in the business. Daily internal and personal course correction can be tracked and monitored to continuously improve in this area of their lives.

The *business* aspect of the 4 B's refers not only to one's occupation, but also all aspects of a person's work in this world. Leaders must nurture their creativity, and work daily toward creating and building not just an occupation, but a vocation. The word vocation comes from the Latin word "to call," and refers to the fact that a person's work is meant to be more than a way to earn money, but to be a purpose-driven calling.

The ancient alchemists had a term called "Magnum Opus" or "The Great Work," which referred to their life's quest to turn lead into gold and find the elixir of life. For each person, this can be different, but it refers to doing the work that they were born to do. As people work daily on the business dimension of their life, they can also seek to move toward fulfilling their "Great Work."

When there is awareness, acknowledgment, and monitoring of these four most important things in a person's life, there is a chance to refine their ways to become better business people and better individuals overall. Find a key item that you can identify as a high-value item for working *in* your business, and give that 1/2 point. Now, really dig deep and wide and identify a "big rock" key item that would be working *on* your business. This is one of those items that would bring big positive change, if you carved out the time to do it daily. Even if just a little bit of that key 'big rock" item were to be done, you would move the dial. This becomes your other 1/2 point in your business, with a focus to get to 1 point a day in your business category. Anything that can be tracked and measured can be improved upon as the 4 B's become a daily way of life. You will start to see quantum shifts in all these key areas of your life. You will also start experiencing the awareness of an even more integrated life, working organically in a more harmonious and joyful way!

Owners and individuals should not shy away from asking, "How am I in every area of my life? Am I giving in? Am I helping or serving others?" Personal mission statements arise out of this. What is their truth? What are their core values? What is their balance sheet on how happy their people are in the business? How happy are they in scoring their own level of happiness and joy? Do they have breakout sessions focused on these subjects? Do they reach out to their customers and clients through surveys? Is their business for-benefit, for-profit, or both?

If owners and leaders are looking to better their company—their experience, recruiting opportunities, employee retention, customer engagement, and client relationships—they would benefit from having trackable and measurable mindsets. This will allow leaders to have a creative environment that allows them to flourish and grow. Tangible results can come out of this. It's not just a feel-good for a few minutes. It's change that impacts their lives, organization, and community, with long-term results.

Important to success with this system is consistency. There is a power that comes from doing a simple task on a consistent basis. Going to the gym sporadically will not bring much change, but going every day for a month will provide real, tangible results. Daily improvements that are too small to notice in the short term, result in massive changes when viewed on a scale of months or even years. By tracking the 4 B's, one can create an accountability system that encourages consistency.

It is different for everyone, but most people find that it takes anywhere from three weeks to three months of consistency to build a habit that "sticks." Tracking the 4 B's is a great way to commit to building crucial habits that are essential for all aspects of health and success. Perhaps after a few months, the practice of daily fulfilling the requirements of the 4 B's will become automatic. You will be surprised at how your weekly score may start initially low, but can swiftly soar to 25, 26, 27.5 or even 28 points a week. This is a great way to track and monitor your progress, growth, and success. The discipline will be so ingrained that you will no longer need to think about it, and falling back into bad habits would be inconceivable.

This will also lead to you becoming aware of your weakest and lower scoring categories. If you start seeing consistent zeros, you will know your goal and stated value in that category is lacking your time, effort, and commitment. There is most likely a deeper-rooted problem holding you back. Much of that can be caused by the lower energy of the ego, not allowing you to complete your goals. However, it is truly something if you commit to sticking with it, as your being will compel you to explore it! I encourage you to follow that nudge and to go on that journey! When individuals take daily inventory of how much they're taking care of their 4 B's, they do finally start finding even more of the right balance in life.

Anything that can be tracked and measured can be improved upon, most importantly, your levels of joy and fulfillment.

We all desire that ourselves and our family be healthy and happy. But at a deeper level than "just happiness" is the level of joy. Happiness can be fleeting as it ebbs and flows with our changing emotions. When you get to a deep level of joy in your life, it truly can permeate every layer of who you are, what you do, and how you show up in the world to others.

Having a big vision, a mission, core values, and a plan for your business and life can make you unstoppable. This plan should be clear and written with conviction. Daily accountability and staying on track with the 4 B's can help you keep the momentum you desire and need. The 4 B's give you the opportunity to course correct swiftly, when the scorecard shows it is needed.

Scan the QR code or use this link to watch the section videos and more on this section topic:
https://steverodgers.net/the-power-of-daily-inventory-and-course-correction

111

#Tracking and #Measuring how much good you're doing daily allows you to invite God or goodness more into your life and business. How many good things are you and everyone in your business doing?

_____

_____

_____

112

Ensure that the 4 B's (your body, your being, your bonds, and your business) are in alignment with the goodness you want to invite into your life. This enables you to know whether your daily actions are directed toward achieving your goals. #4B's

_____

_____

_____

113

Anything you can #TrackAndMeasure, you can improve upon. Spend time tracking and measuring how much you're taking care of your body, your being, your bonds, and your business. #4B's

_____

_____

_____

114

Determine what good you want to do for your body (e.g., eat healthy, exercise, etc.) and track if you're doing that daily. #Body

_____

_____

_____

115

Are you praying or meditating daily? #TrackAndMeasure how much you're bettering your being in order to create a closer connection/relationship with God (or a higher power). #Being

_____

_____

_____

116

#TrackAndMeasure your bonds or relationships.
Start with your immediate family. Are you spending
time deepening your bond with your husband,
wife, siblings, sons, or daughters? #Bonds

_____

_____

_____

117

Successful business owners and leaders are those who
work IN their business and ON their business. Are you
working in and on your business? #Business

_____

_____

_____

118

Determine your goals and destination, be ready for the journey, push off from the dock, and set sail. #TrackAndMeasure

_____

_____

_____

119

If you're unable to work on bettering your body, your being, your bonds, or your business, don't wonder why some things in your life and business are not doing well. #CourseCorrect yourself after a day vs a week.

_____

_____

_____

120

Having a scorecard that you can use to #TrackAndMeasure how much you're bettering your body, your being, your bonds, and your business is a good tool that can help you invite more goodness into your life and your business.

_____

_____

121

#Tracking and #Measuring one's body, being, bonds, and business can be a fun exercise for your employees. This can become a friendly competition that enables happiness, fulfillment, and success in their lives both at home and at work.

_____

_____

_____

122

Diligent, consistent, focused effort toward a goal can result in great achievements. #Goals

_____

_____

_____

123

The more you #TrackAndMeasure how much good you're doing in your life, the more you can improve. The more you can improve, the more God (or a higher power) becomes visible in your life and guides you to success.

_____

_____

_____

"Prayer is you speaking to God. Meditation is allowing the spirit to speak to you."
—Deepak Chopra

Steve Rodgers
https://aha.pub/IGIPrinciples

At the very end of this section, share the AHA messages from this book socially by going to **https://aha.pub/IGIPrinciples**.

Section VIII

The Power of Breath, Prayer, and Meditation

To live in the modern world is to feel tremendous pressure to produce, achieve, and succeed. In all this activity and self-centered striving, people lose touch with a deeper intelligence. Deeper intelligence is found in silence, listening, and trust in their intuition. Likewise, in business, many individuals often feel too constricted by the bottom line to relax and allow creativity to flourish.

Business owners and leaders who want joy, fulfillment, and success, would be greatly aided in this pursuit by *Inviting GOodness In*-to their lives and businesses. But how does one open up to allow that goodness in? How does one attend to hectic schedules in business, family affairs, and responsibilities and still manage to care for their own inner person?

This section talks about how breath, prayer, and meditation can help. These are well-known practices in personal lives but often underappreciated in the business world. With many things going on in business every day, leaders have a responsibility to take action and inspire everyone to *Invite GOodness In*.

It's sincerely a gift to just be able to breathe every day. Truly, our first and most important gift of any waking day, each breath, is a reminder to be "present in the present moment." When things get hectic and busy, breathing exercises can help generate calm. In our lives, we only have a limited number of breaths, a limited number of days that we can experience the miracle of inhaling oxygen, life's secret force, and feeling sustained by it. So why not make the best of each breath that we are blessed with? Being alive and being able to breathe—naturally and effortlessly—can help owners and leaders appreciate life more, and to be present at all times. At times these things are taken for granted. When a person can hear themselves breathe, they are more aware of their own presence and of nature around them.

The breath is one of the most simple and powerful ways in which we can bring ourselves into the present moment and find peace. Moreover, it does not require taking any special breaks or buying special equipment. It can be practiced simultaneously while working on a project, talking with clients, in a meeting, or in the midst of doing anything. By anchoring themselves with their breath, individuals can bring a deep awareness of their physical body and reminded to stay present in the moment.

Just the act of catching yourself enough, to know you want to change your state, is a key superpower. You can then magnify this superpower many times over. Under any circumstances you can stop your thoughts, shift the rate or depth of your breath, and use a mantra with conscious breathing. This will create an immediate sense of peace and a new state awareness. Even if it is only a few seconds, sometimes that is all it takes.

A few mantras and affirmations I have used for years are the following:

- "I am the stillness in the storm"
- "I am the calm in the chaos"
- "Be the bringer of the light, you are that, so be it."
- God grant me the serenity... you can easily just flow into the short but powerful serenity prayer.

I often repeat these multiple times in my head, or even out loud. I do it as I am in full awareness of my breath and consciously changing my mental and emotional state. You can practice this as you walk into any potentially stressful situation. You would be surprised how quickly it works. Furthermore, the more you do it, the faster the act goes on auto-pilot, sometimes clicking on before you even realize it's been activated.

Praying is a choice. Most people pray because they believe that there is something or someone outside of themselves. They seek refuge in a higher power to give thanks for their blessings, to share fears and hopes, and to ask for something the heart or soul needs and desires. The courage to move forward is found when they can talk to someone—a higher being—with whom they can trust their deepest thoughts. Prayer can be as simple as a whisper, or a lengthy utterance of words with petition and supplication to *Invite Good In*, to praise and give thanksgiving, or to ask forgiveness. It can be a number of things to different people. Praying is like inviting the universal energy—an expression of God, good, greatness, or grace—into their lives, which essentially all points to the Creator or the sum of all energy.

Just like anything else, prayer can be used to either *Edge God Out* or *Invite God In*. When prayer is a petition for material possessions and success, it is coming from ego. However, when an individual opens themselves up to listening to the wisdom of a higher power, and how they can align themselves with that higher power, they are coming from IGI. True prayer is not asking for something that will strengthen the ego; it is opening up a dialogue between the individual and the universe, and humbly opening themselves to guidance.

When praying, it humbles an individual and reminds them that they can't do things all on their own. It helps them realize that they are co-creators and all people coexist in this relationship with one another. How consciously they are doing this may determine how strong their inner person is. If God is bold enough to be involved in the business of money, how does God (or goodness) show up in their lives? Praying is like being in a relationship, where they must not only think about themselves, but also about the other person. What will affect that relationship when making decisions, for example? The power of God (or the higher being they believe in) is manifested in their personal lives and in business through a commitment to the relationship and prayer. Get creative and make your own mantra. Try whatever combination of positive words and images comes from your imagination and works best for you.

For me, this relationship with God, what I choose to call my higher power, has become the most intimate and consistent relationship in my life. This relationship is above all others; above even my wife, with whom I have shared thirty joyful years of marriage. Making my relationship with the higher power my priority, has been much of the reason we both have sustained and grown through our relationship here on earth.

The creator source-energy is where I aim and strive to be connected to in all things, at all hours, every day. Prayer and meditation help me to connect and be reminded of that most important sacred relationship.

Meditation is being still in both mind and body. The human mind constantly has chatter, which can cause uneasiness and anxiety. Meditation helps clear the mind and make it peaceful. It can clear the mind of unnecessary noise, things that can cause burnout but can be avoided.

Even taking five minutes out of the day to sit silently and observe all that is happening within, and without, can be a powerful practice. Simply sit in a relaxed, yet alert, position with a straight spine and be fully present in one's breathing. Taking this time to sit and contact the inner being can help in bringing that presence into everyday life.

Some businesses have successfully incorporated breath, prayer, and meditation in their culture, and actually encourage these practices in the workplace. There are sleep pods, chapels, and areas for rest, for employees to regroup and revive their stamina and energy. These practices help improve decision-making for leaders and owners to regain their mental strength and power of thinking. They offer yoga classes, nutrition classes, and even breathing breaks. IGI-oriented leaders can help their employees reduce stress by placing positive and productive activities in the workplace. This helps everyone function better and be happier at work.

Not only are these meditative practices great for health and personal wellbeing, but they also have a utilitarian value. Individuals are able to relax, re-charge, and center themselves through a yoga or meditation break. They can then bring the benefits of this into their work throughout the day. Personal experiences, as well as scientific studies, clearly prove that taking even just twenty minutes out of a workday to engage in wellness practices, leads to better quality work in the long run.

Successful and effective owners and leaders allow their employees to express their home stresses, health challenges, and spiritual and religious beliefs. This allows people to be their whole selves within the business, which results in better morale, better retention, potentially more profits, and a happier workforce.

Business leaders who incorporate breath, prayer, and meditation in their business can help everyone invite more goodness in. These things are teachable, trackable, and measurable.

Incorporating breath, prayer, and meditation in the workplace can help everyone become more connected to goodness and positivity. Those things allow your business to do more good and drive well-rounded success. Even more, they are some of the most effective ways to aid an individual in connecting to their inner being, where they can find guidance, fulfillment, and purpose in life.

A daily mantra that can be used when faced with a decision is to ask: "Am I in ego or IGI?" This brings the mind back to what is truly important, back to one's inner orientation. Taking a moment to be inwardly silent through breathing, meditation, or prayer and tuning in to the energy behind one's actions, is a constant reminder to act in IGI.

Scan the QR code or use this link to watch the section videos and more on this section topic:
https://steverodgers.net/the-power-of-breath-prayer-and-meditation

124

Breathing, prayer, and meditation are the strongest connections you can have with God (or a higher power). The stronger your connection to that higher power, the more you open yourself up to goodness.

_____

_____

_____

125

Breathing, praying and meditation can allow you to make better decisions for your business and your employees, which helps them have a happier and more fulfilling work environment.

_____

_____

_____

126

Every breath we take is a gift from God. It's a reminder that you are alive and that you have no other choice but to #BePresent in the moment. Are you being present? #BusinessSuccess

_____

_____

_____

127

One of the biggest keys to successfully focusing on
our purpose and our passion is to learn to live in the
moment. #BePresent

_____

_____

_____

128

The more we can be fully present in the present,
the more effective we will be in each moment in time.
#BePresent

_____

_____

_____

129

Everything in your life, whether it be praying or meditating, is something you can choose to do or not to do. Breathing is something that we all do automatically, but how we honor each and every breath is key.
#BePresent

130

Breathing can help you control your body, your stress, and your anxiety, which allows you to channel your energy and your focus on your work. When things are getting hectic in the business, remember to #Breathe. #BusinessSuccess

131

Praying is people acknowledging that there is something higher than themselves, that they're speaking to something higher with solution consciousness, and that they can share their concerns, fears, wishes, hopes, and desires.

_____

_____

_____

132

Meditation is where you're being still and calming your mind. Our minds are constantly full of chatter, and meditating helps drown the chatter and provides us with peace of mind.

_____

_____

_____

133

Your managers and employees are human, and they feel stress at home and at work. Offer them a way that can help reduce their stress so they can function better and live better lives.

_____

_____

_____

134

Introducing breathing, prayer, and meditation to your managers and employees can help your business function better. The better your managers and employees are performing, the better your chances of achieving #BusinessSuccess.

_____

_____

_____

135

Create a space in your business that helps better the body, mind, and spirit of your managers and employees (e.g., having yoga classes or a meditation room), in order to bring more happiness, which can drive more engagement and creativity.

_____

_____

_____

136

Many businesses incorporate meditation and yoga in their organizations to allow everyone to nourish their bodies and souls. When people in businesses are nourished, they become more energized and productive.

_____

_____

_____

137

Help your managers and employees find a substitute for bad, addictive behavior. Introduce something more addictive, but that can bring positive results in their lives, such as breathing exercises, yoga, meditation, and prayer.

_____

_____

_____

138

Aside from paying good wages, help nourish your managers' and employees' hearts and souls. This can potentially result in better morale, better retention, more profits, and a happier workforce.

_____

_____

_____

139

Successful business owners and leaders incorporate breathing, prayer, and meditation into their businesses for the purpose of bettering people's lives. When you help better someone's life, you better your own life, too.

_____

_____

_____

140

Breathing, prayer, and meditation allow you to open yourself up to God's (or other higher power's) guidance to do good and achieve success both in life and in business.

_____

_____

_____

.

Conclusion

In my opinion, IGI and the principles that it stands for, is an idea whose time has come. As individuals, and the world at large, are hungering for a deeper experience of being in their professional lives and to find their purpose. All while doing work that benefits their bank accounts, their souls, planet and all beings.

In our world, we have seen many movements and revolutions that reflect the underlying consciousness of the people. The Enlightenment in the 17th century was the result of a growing critical mass of individuals who believed in reason, liberty, and the scientific method. This shift in consciousness had a deep impact on human civilization that is still felt today.

Now, in the auspicious year of 2020, the signs are growing clearer, roaring louder, and in some ways screaming: **We are in another age of transformation**, in which more and more people are seeking to leave behind old beliefs in separation, inequality, and intolerance. We are begging to integrate a holistic sense of Spiritual Intelligence and greater consciousness into our lives and businesses.

With the interconnected nature of our society due to the internet and social media, I see vast potential for spiritual consciousness, and Spiritual Intelligence to go viral. In fact, I see signs that it is already happening.

There are more and more people who are seeking positivity, personal growth, and happiness. As a critical mass of individuals step forward who value truth and fairness, wanting a better life for themselves, their families, and the future of many generations to come. They are no longer asking, but are demanding to be heard and make a difference.

We are all being pulled back to our true nature and drawn forward to our divine potential. We are all seeking not just happiness, but a deeper joy as we are seen, accepted, and live a life of value. The ultimate nirvana of being of service with your God-given gifts, is a reality for each and everyone one of us!

My vision and dream is that the essence of IGI will become a worldwide movement, in the business world especially, but also in all domains. People do not need to necessarily use the word "IGI", although it is a catchy and easy to remember mantra that is a nice contrast to ego. Instead of "getting jiggy wit it", you can remind yourself to "get IGI with it!" As long as you are following the spirit of inviting goodness and grace into your life, the word you use for this doesn't matter.

IGI can stand for whatever you wish it to be. It can be *Inviting God In*, *Inviting Good In*, *Inviting Grace In*, *Inviting Greatness In*, or any other G-word you can think of!

IGI, *Inviting GOodness In*, is just one of many ways to describe the practice of ceasing to live solely in EGO, *Edging God Out*. EGO creates a state of consciousness that is based in separation, fear, greed, and a belief in lack, which causes one's life to become a constant effort to protect and bolster a false self.

The ego is of the material world and our earthly existence, and therefore has a positive side as an essential part of our physical existence. It is not going away, and as long as we are in this realm, we need it to survive and have the energy to take action. It does have a very important purpose - sometimes we just need to get shit done!

Spiritual Intelligence is developing the skills to learn how to integrate both ego and IGI, while allowing IGI to lead. It is the alchemy of the two that you will instinctually follow when you learn to practice IGI each moment of every day. Doing this, goodness leaks into your heart and soul. The operating system of your consciousness is upgraded to a newer version that will best serve you, others, and the world. Forge that path, and you will uncover your own power that will serve God and Good at levels that you never thought possible.

When we begin to live in IGI, we realize that the fulfillment, security, success, and love we deeply desire, are not found through gaining possessions and prestige. The things we desire out of life are found within, by opening ourselves up to a greater consciousness of ourselves and our connection to life, the universe, and our higher power. This fundamental change in one's orientation and identity radically transforms all aspects of your life.

This is truly where the sweetness of life becomes even sweeter. Simultaneously, the bitterness we all taste and experience will become a new tolerable flavor that you can define in a whole new way. The trials of life will become a new friend you never knew you wanted or needed. Your daily perspective will shift in ways you did not notice or see before, and the black and white parts of life you used to see will now start having more added color.

You will begin to see the version of you that you always hoped and expected the world to see unfold in the eyes of those you meet - and more importantly, in front of yours. Peace and purpose will find you, not just in spurts, but in your daily, beautiful life.

At this time on our Earth, the old religions are being more and more challenged to adapt to the modern world. The definition of what it means to be religious or spiritual is broadening to include an eclectic mix of traditions and beliefs from all over the world, as individuals create their own spiritual philosophy and practice that works for them. IGI embraces this kind of individual self-creation, as each person discovers how to best invite goodness into their lives.

Spirituality today must be inclusive, not exclusive. You can still have your personal beliefs and spiritual practices. You can be Catholic, Jewish, or Muslim, but you don't have to ascribe to any formal religious system. The point is to be an individual but still also be part of a collective whole, in society and the world. Finding connectivity by being of service, by doing well, by doing good and by giving to others. This then becomes your unique personal religion or spirituality - however you wish to define that.

"I am not a human being having a spiritual experience, I am a spiritual being having a human experience" I first came to know of this quote through Wayne Dyer.

I love this quote because this succinctly expresses the truth that the spiritual dimension underlies our entire existence and experience in this life. As human beings, we can no longer divorce the spiritual dimension of life from the rest of our experience.

The IGI Principles are one way that an individual can discover their unique gifts, and share them with the world as a spiritual being in this human experience. In this way, you are allowed to be the true you, that you were created to be, while also being a part of a worldwide movement. A movement of individuals in all spheres of work and business, who are allowing their Spiritual Intelligence to infuse their creative output in the world.

Humanity and the Earth are being rapidly transformed, as more and more individuals are taking action in their lives. Actions for the sake of higher consciousness, for the good of their community, the benefit of their business, and for themselves. I look forward to a bright future where IGI principles are ubiquitous in all forms of business.

A challenge for many is integrating these principles, and this new Spiritual Intelligence, into their business and work. That is the purpose of this book, and I hope it has offered you valuable, actionable guidance on just how to do that in your own life.

This is just the introductory volume of what I anticipate to be many more books in the IGI series. In further books, I will explore more deeply how *Inviting GOodness In* can offer guidance on how to be incorporated and transformative in your life. Additionally, I will continue to release videos, blog articles, and other daily content online to help inspire you on your own IGI journey.

I look forward to working with you to see how you can apply the principles into your own life and business, to achieve your purpose, and contribute to a better world for all.

I invite you to join me on this joyful journey to live in your own IGI state of mind and being.

Scan the QR code or use this link to watch the call to action video: https://steverodgers.net/conclusion

IGI Ambassadors

Here, I'd like to acknowledge individuals who have supported me in my work and whom I would encourage my readers to look into. Each one of them has a unique perspective and gifts to share, and I have been greatly nourished by their friendship and support. These are all inspiring individuals living their own version of IGI in the world and supporting a better world for all. They have all contributed in one way or another to the manifestation of the book, and I would like to take the opportunity here to highlight and honor them. I encourage readers of this book to learn more about these individuals' missions, messages, and offerings and how you can connect with them.

Allyn Reid
Allyn is an author and co-founder of the Secret of Happiness and the Secret Knock workshops. Allyn is also a publisher, producer, and Mrs. San Diego 2015.
https://about.me/allynreid

Andrew Hewitt
For more than a decade, Andrew has been uniting the GameChangers of our time to evolve economics and address the systemic challenges we face. In 2010, Andrew set out on a mission to showcase a new standard of success in business, which led to the publication of GameChangers 500, a ranking of the world's top mission-driven businesses.
https://gamechangers.co

Barnet G. Meltzer, MD, FAAFP
Barnet is a pioneer and expert physician in holistic and preventative medicine, as well as an author, talk show host, and speaker.
http://www.maketimeforwellness.com

Bill Walsh
Bill is the CEO and founder of Power Team USA and has been voted as one of the top ten business coaches in the US by Global Gurus.
http://www.ipowerteam.com

Brandon Barnum

A seasoned expert with visionary leadership, Brandon has been building tech companies for over twenty-three years. Most recently, he was co-founder and president of Refer.com (now Pod.io), the world's largest referral network of over five million members in over 180 countries. Brandon is now the Chairman of the Board of HOA.com and can be found at
www.elevatingperformance.com

Brian S. Tracy

Brian is an amazing mentor and friend, is a world-renowned speaker, a writer of over seventy bestselling books, has consulted for more than 1,000 companies, and addressed more than 5,000,000 people in 5,000 talks and seminars throughout the world.
www.briantracy.com

Cheri Tree

Cheri is creator and owner of the revolutionary B.A.N.K. methodology and Codebreaker's Personality Coding Technology, designed to help business owners close more sales in less time and improve their communication skills and personal relationships.
https://www.cheritree.com

David M. Corbin

David is a coach, keynote speaker, business adviser, and author of *ILLUMINATE*, *Preventing Brand Slaughter*, and *ReSanity*. He has been referred to as, "Robin Williams with an MBA," because of his practical, high-relevant content speeches coupled with entertaining and sometimes side-splitting stories. He has served as management and leadership consultant to businesses and organizations of all sizes—from Fortune 20 companies to businesses with less than 1 million—and enjoys the challenges of all.
http://davidcorbin.com

David Tal and Avi Tal

David and Avi are brothers and former real estate executives and marketing pros who in 2015, co-founded Agentology, now known as Verse, a platform that assists clients in all business sectors engage, qualify, and convert inbound leads.
https://verse.io

Edward Krifcher
Eddy co-owns and operates the Keller Williams Forward Living real estate offices in Los Angeles doing 10,000 transactions a year. He also owns and operates the Keller Williams offices in Pittsburgh, is a co-owner of ClearMark Title, as well as numerous escrow companies. He is also a serial entrepreneur and a very savvy real estate investor.

Eric Lochtefeld
Eric is co-founder of the life changing mastermind Bliss Champions with Patrick Combs. He lives his Bliss by helping others win at theirs. As a Blisspreneur, he starts and invests in businesses that begin as secret or unrealized ambitions that transform into great businesses.
https://www.ericlochtefeld.com https://www.blisschampions.com

Esther Wildenberg
Esther is the CEO and co-founder scratch EVP of Global sales at BANKCODE. She is also a keynote speaker, executive business coach, sales trainer, leadership retreat facilitator, and entrepreneur.
http://bankicon.com

Greg S. Reid
Greg is the author of "Three Feet From Gold", the "Think and Grow Rich" series, as well as countless other books. He is also President of Blue Sky consulting, leads the Secret Knock Workshops and is a serial entrepreneur, and sought after speaker. He is also a movie producer, his most recent film being "Wish Man". www.secretknock.co www.gregreid.com

Haris Reis
Haris is a National #1 Best-Selling Author, President of Zenfusion and The Gamechangers Academy, and CEO of BIH Media Inc.
http://www.harisreis.com

Jessica Rhodes she is the founder at Interview Connections
Jessica is the leading expert on how to leverage podcast guesting for increased brand awareness, more leads, and higher profits. She created the podcast booking industry in 2013, when she founded Interview Connections, the first and leading agency of its kind. They are podcast experts and the top podcast booking service.
http://www.interviewconnections.com

Jim Bunch

Jim is the Co-founder & President of The Ultimate Game of Life and co-founder and president at Powur, the first clean energy technology platform that is disrupting and decentralizing the way the world uses energy.
https://powur.com/ http://www.jimbunch.com/who/bio.html

John Assaraf

John is chairman and CEO of NeuroGym, contributed to the book, *The Secret*, and has written *The Answer*, *Having It All*, and various other bestselling books. John is also a sought out speaker, frequent TV show guest and serial entrepreneur.
https://johnassaraf.com www.myneurogym.com

Dr. Ken Druck

Ken's pioneering work over the past forty years as an author, speaker, thought leader, executive coach, consultant, and community leader is encapsulated under the heading: "Courageous Living." Courageous Living is the decision to face, rather than turn away from, life's greatest challenges and to create your best possible future. Whether you are summoning the courage to overcome adversity or harvest an opportunity, you'll find tools to get you there from Ken's offerings.
https://www.kendruck.com/

Leon Logothetis

Leon is a global adventurer, TV host, motivational speaker, and best-selling author. For over a decade, he's traveled the globe to over 100 countries to highlight the good in humanity. As documented through his best-selling books and TV shows, Leon works constantly to inspire the world with his message of kindness and hope. This is best shown through his Netflix series, *The Kindness Diaries*.
https://www.leonlogothetis.com

Mark C. Thompson

Mark is a *NY Times* bestselling author, Serial Midas touch investor, and former chief of staff at Charles Schwab. He has worked side by side with Steve Jobs, Charles Schwab, and Richard Branson. Mark is a Broadway producer as well as in very high demand for international keynote speaking and consulting.
http://markcthompson.com

Marshall Goldsmith

Marshal was voted into the Top 5 Executive Business Coach Global Gurus Thinkers 50 list and is a *NY Times* bestselling author of *Triggers, MOJO,* and *What Got You Here, Won't Get You There.* He has also founded the Coaches 100 group that is paying good deeds forward all over the world!
http://www.marshallgoldsmithgroup.com

Mitchell Levy

Global Credibility Expert Mitchell Levy is a TEDx speaker and international bestselling author of over sixty books. A general theme heard from the clients he's ghost-written books for and the hundreds of thought leaders he's created credreels for is that he's "unconsciously competent at clarifying your message." He's an accomplished entrepreneur who has created twenty businesses in Silicon Valley, including four publishing companies that have published over 850 books. He's provided strategic consulting to hundreds of companies and has been chairman of the board of a NASDAQ-listed company.
https://AHAthat.com

Niurka

For the last two decades, Niurka has been creating and leading transformational experiences that improve and enrich people's businesses, relationships, and lives. She's guided hundreds of thousands of people to elevate the way they think, speak, and live. After being a top global trainer for Tony Robbins Niurka launched her company in 2000 with a vision of Inspiring Social Transformation through Inner Evolution. She has customized training curriculums for many of the most powerful companies in the world who have produced record-breaking results by applying her teachings.
https://www.niurkainc.com

Patrick Combs

Patrick has shared his stories and strategies with millions of people around the globe for twenty-five years and his one man show is now being made into a movie. He's a top-rated book author, widely known motivational speaker, and thought leader on passion, possibility, and heart-based business. Patrick is also co-founder of the life changing mastermind Bliss Champions with Eric Lochtefeld.
http://www.patrickcombs.com/ https://www.blisschampions.com

Paul Morris
Paul is Keller Williams' Regional Owner Director for three California Regions, where he has oversight of thirty-six offices and more than 7,000 realtors who close more than $18 billion in sales volume per year. As a prolific, award-winning entrepreneur and business mind, Paul continues to grow and impact the real estate industry. He is also a prior *New York Times* bestselling author of *Wealth Can't Wait*.
http://www.morrisx.com, www.wealth.org

Rich German
Rich is the author of *Monetize Your Passion* and co-founder of the JV Experience. He is also a top coach and a sea-life lover and advocate.
http://richgerman.com

Dr. Scott and Shannon Peck
Scott and Shannon are Love Master teachers, speakers, & co-authors of many books on love & healing, the authors of *The Love You Deserve* and *Liberating Your Magnificence*. Scott has also been a seasoned real estate professional at the very top of his field for many years and Shannon is a skilled healer and past life regression counselor.
http://www.scottandshannonpeck.com/bio

Steven E. Schmitt
Steven is the founder of the Law of Positivity, as well as an author, entrepreneur, and media expert. He successfully leads people to reach millions with their work and messages.
https://www.bestsellerguru.com/sell-millions-of-books

"P.S. Don't forget to watch the videos at the end of each chapter. They will give you more direct perspective from the author. Also make sure you check out the links to the AHA Messages web page. You will find thousands more there from other amazing people on a very wide range of valuable topics!"

"Individuality doesn't just mean individualism - standing alone. It means developing one's unique gifts, and being able to share them for the enjoyment of oneself and others."
—Frances Moore Lappé

Steve Rodgers
https://aha.pub/IGIPrinciples

Appendix

Thank you for going on this journey through the IGI Principles with me. I hope that you have enjoyed this book and found value that you can apply in your life starting today.

On this page are collected in one place all the videos for each section of the book. You can continue to revisit this page to watch and re-watch the videos as many times as you need to imbibe their message.

Call to Action
https://steverodgers.net/call-to-action/

Introduction
https://steverodgers.net/introduction/

Foreword by Mark C. Thompson
https://steverodgers.net/foreword-by-mark-thompson/

Section I: Inviting Good In VS Edging Good Out
https://steverodgers.net/inviting-good-in-vs-edging-good-out/

Section II: The Power of Gratitude
https://steverodgers.net/the-power-of-gratitude/

Section III: The Power of Forgiveness
https://steverodgers.net/the-power-of-forgiveness/

Section IV: Living Up to Your Moral Fiber and Choosing to Do The Right Thing
https://steverodgers.net/living-up-to-your-moral-fiber-and-choosing-to-do-the-right-thing/

Section V: The Power of Being of Service and Paying It Forward
https://steverodgers.net/the-power-of-being-of-service-and-paying-it-forward/

Section VI: Letting Go and Turning Things Over to Trust
https://steverodgers.net/letting-go-and-turning-things-over-to-trust/

Section VII: The Power of Daily Inventory and Course Correction—The 4 B's
https://steverodgers.net/the-power-of-daily-inventory-and-course-correction/

Section VIII: The Power of Breath, Prayer, and Meditation
https://steverodgers.net/the-power-of-breath-prayer-and-meditation/

Conclusion:
https://steverodgers.net/conclusion/

About the Author

Steve Rodgers, author of Amazon #1 bestselling book, *Lead to Gold*, and creator of Alchemy Advisors coaching and consulting firm, is a former Warren Buffett CEO who experienced a radical spiritual transformation that has evolved into a new mission as a purpose-driven consultant and entrepreneur coach, in-demand international keynote speaker, and bestselling author.

A Spiritual Business Activist, Steve specializes in helping business owners and leaders increase profits while bringing spiritual intelligence into every aspect of their personal and professional lives to invite in success, fulfillment, and abundance beyond their wildest dreams. He shows how you can create personal success while also serving others and the world as a whole.

He recognizes himself as a spiritual being having a human experience whose purpose is to help individuals discover their purpose and maximize their highest good in life and business.

Steve lives near San Diego with his wife and dog. When not coaching and consulting, he enjoys bike riding, yoga, meditation, and spending time with his children and grandchildren.

Visit my website www.steverodgers.net to connect with me and continue your IGI journey.

AHAthat®

THiNKaha has created AHAthat for you to share content from this book.

- ➲ Share each AHA message socially: **https://aha.pub/IGIPrinciples**
- ➲ Share additional content: **https://AHAthat.com**
- ➲ Info on authoring: **https://AHAthat.com/Author**

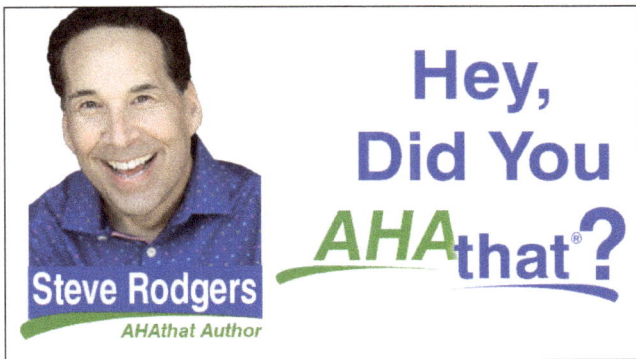

Steve Rodgers
AHAthat Author

Hey, Did You AHAthat®?

www.ingramcontent.com/pod-product-compliance
Lightning Source LLC
Chambersburg PA
CBHW042117190326
41519CB00030B/7525